A Breath of Fresh God

A Breath of Fresh God

Charissa Fryberger

Kha'ris Books

2021

ISBN: 978–1–7363917–4–7

Cover Design by Jenna Yeager
Cover Photo by Charissa Fryberger:
  Squirrel Creek Trail, Beulah, Colorado.
Breath Grapic by Annette Meserve Lucero
Back cover portrait by Mollie Hitt

This book is lovingly dedicated
to my husband, David,
who invited me to meet Christ,
taught me to live in His peace,
and has shared with me
in an intriguing and exhilarating
odyssey of life and faith.

Jesus Lingers . . .

Take a breath…
and another.

Feel a stirring in the air:
a whisper,
a fragrance,
a sigh on the breeze.

Breathe.
Breathe again.
Breathe deeply.

God is near.

. . . Emmanuel.

Table of Contents

Introduction: Ahh, a Breath of Fresh . . .   1

Ways to Read *A Breath of Fresh God*   6

Take a breath . . .   9

Abba   10

The Augustinian Ant   12

Distracted   16

And another . . .   18

Before the King (*an imagining*)   19

Rivers of Living Water   24

The Gallery   28

A stirring . . .   34

Eight Billion Pixels   35

Letters from Abroad   40

Ты or Вы?   56

A whisper . . .   63

Trip Report: Pikes Peak   64

Raw Deal   73

Cancer, Comfort, and Calling   77

A fragrance . . .   82

To Be or Not To Be the Blind Man   83

The Author   88

The Song of a Lonely King *(an imagining)*   90

A sigh . . .   104

In the Playroom *(an imagining)*   105

The Strong Nuclear Force   109

An Audience with the King   114

Breakfast   121

The Master's Move   124

Breathe . . .   127

What If . . . ?   128

Bored with Miracles   138

Too Many Shades of Blue   140

Breathe again . . .   146

Malchus   147

When the Extraordinary Fits   153

Acceleration   159

Breathe deeply . . .   162

A Magnum Opus   163

Naked and Unashamed   168

Forget the Fig Leaves   170

God is Near . . .   176

At 13,000 Feet   178

Walls Soaked in Prayer   183

The Chalice   186

An Invitation to Dine (*an imagining*)   189

Emmanuel . . .   202

Questions and Activities   207

Recommended Readings   246

Thank you!   247

Patron's Page   251

About the Author   252

Timeline of Writings   254

A Breath of Fresh God

Introduction:
Ahh, a Breath of Fresh...

When we open a window and inhale the cool breeze outside, "Ah," we say, "A breath of fresh air!" Its pleasant relief from the stuffiness in the room gives us a whole new outlook on the day. We breathe deeply.

In reality, the air isn't fresh or new. It hasn't changed at all. It is still the same atmosphere that has surrounded our home all evening; we just needed to open the window to become aware of it. Did we know the fresh air was out there? Of course. If we had thought the air had receded, we would have been justifiably panicked. Rather, we have been busy with a myriad of other tasks and concerns and have forgotten to stop and take a breath.

And so it is with God. He is always out there, surrounding us on all sides, but we get sidetracked with the distractions that catch us, the pleasures that entice us, the obligations that pull on us, and we forget to notice Him. Then our spirits become stuffy and stale. We don't even register our discomfort until some tiny movement outside the glass catches our attention. We stop to open the window and look out.

Just one breath of fresh God changes our perspective

and brightens our day. It can be inspired by a word from a friend, a line from a song, the scent of a blooming lilac bush floating on the breeze, or the laughter of a child on a swing.

This book is filled with breaths—divine sighs portrayed in images and word pictures that attempt, however awkwardly, to help us explore who this God really is.

We worship a God we cannot see. We can be aware of His Presence all around us, but we cannot point Him out and say, "Look, there He is." We recognize Him in the breaths that float past us and the fingerprints He leaves for us to find. We describe those indescribable touches in symbols and word pictures; in metaphors and images that help us think about and convey our brushes with the Divine. These symbolic portraits make it possible for us to comprehend the incomprehensible and imagine the unimaginable.

The Bible offers us many images of God. He is called the Shepherd as well as the Lamb. He is Father and Son. He is the Vine; the Lion; both the King and the Servant. He is the Judge and the Savior. He is, in fact, all of these things…and He is none of them. While each provides us with a tiny picture—a window into God's character—none of those windows is big enough for us to see the vast totality of who He is. All of our many symbols ultimately prove to be inadequate.

One of my students emailed me a group picture. Being somewhat technically challenged, I didn't know why this happened (or how to fix it), but the picture appeared on my screen so big that I could barely see one of the twenty-three people in the photo. I could scroll across and down to see it bit by bit, but I could not get a view of the whole picture, nor could it communicate the full sense or character of the event where it was taken.

Our verbal images of God are much the same, each showing us a piece which is, in fact, part of God's character, but which cannot in any way contain or communicate all that He is. No single metaphor can picture Him; even an intricate analogy cannot encompass Him. Each new description provides just one more facet of who He is. Still, these images are valuable in helping us find ways to relate to our God, who is so far beyond our comprehension that we can never know all of Him. By examining and considering these tiny images, we become more acquainted with the God who is both inexpressibly mysterious and, at the same time, so intimately close that He inhabits our very breath.

Is it possible that in struggling with the inadequacies of our language as we try vainly to communicate what it is like to sit at His feet, to lay in His arms, to feel His Hand upon us, we find ourselves understanding our own experience of Him more fully? Even in asking that question, I have fallen again into metaphors: I am sitting at the feet of a God who has no feet and who doesn't need to walk on them because He is everywhere at once; I am lying in the arms of a God whose arms, if He had need of such appendages, would be far too vast for me to cuddle into; I am imagining a moment of intimate caress from a God whose overwhelming Presence touches me on all sides in every moment of every day. Yet each of these insufficient images does describe something I have experienced and crave to experience again and again. Can we even remember and ponder what happened in those sweet times of indefinable communion if we don't assign words and images that attempt to describe those soul-satisfying moments?

A Breath of Fresh God invites you to explore with me the many facets of God's character as we discover in ourselves a greater capacity to delight in the embrace of both the Sustainer of all we know and all we will never know, and the Papa who gently lifts our faces to look into our eyes and gather our tears into His hand.

Hmmm...perhaps I need yet another analogy even to express what I wish to accomplish in the following pages.

My husband and I are fourteener climbers (in our home state of Colorado, fifty-four peaks rise to an elevation of 14,000 feet above sea level or more). When we climb a mountain, we do not climb straight up its face. In most cases such a climb would be impossible; at best it would be dangerous and exhausting. Rather, we follow the trail for many more miles than the actual distance between our outset and the summit, switchbacking back and forth or circling the rocky mass in search of climbable rocks and hikeable ridges. Sometimes we can see the rocky prominence at the top and get a glimpse of the goal. Other times it disappears behind a nearer outcropping, only to reappear further up the trail from an entirely different angle.

By the time we summit, we have looked at the mountain from a thousand viewpoints; we have seen it from far off and from close enough to put out a hand and touch its steep face. Its topography no longer appears as just a point poking into the sky, but rather as a myriad of crevasses and ledges; terrifying drop-offs and solid rocks the size of skyscrapers; trickling streams and snowfields that never melt, even in the heat of July. From the peak, we can look back at the trail and know that we have become acquainted with the mountain in a whole new way.

This is how I want to consider our simultaneously omnipotent and intimate God: gazing up at Him from far below, navigating the ups and downs and ins and outs of His personality and His relationship to us, and reaching out to touch His face.

Among the writings in this book are essays and observations, imaginings drawn from between the lines of Scripture and of life, poems, images, letters, musings, trip reports, and analogies. Some of these pieces wonder at the face of God; others ask Him, and us, hard questions; still others peer behind the scenes of scriptural stories in search of "What if?"

Interspersed among these writings are "breaths"—short italic scenes written in the present tense and designed to remind us all to stop and notice that God is, indeed, here.

The pieces in this book were written at different times and places throughout the United States and around the globe. They appear in neither chronological nor geographical order. Rather, they move from one view of God to another in an attempt to explore His many faces and facets. It is my hope that in these pages we will encounter the King of kings and the joyously celebrating Father of the prodigal—one inviting us into the majesty of His throne room; the other enthusiastically welcoming us as His children. We will peer through metaphorical windows to discover the Master of the universe and the Beloved who wraps us in His arms; the Creator of all we've ever seen and the intimate Friend with whom we can share our deepest secrets. We will find God fulfilling the roles of the Tailor, the Author, the Lover, the Protector, the General, the Gambler, the Chess Master, the Artist, and many others.

And I hope that now and then, a particular phrase or idea will jump off the page, or an image will stick in your mind and make you catch your breath as it suddenly brings you a clearer awareness of His Presence right here next to you . . .

. . . a breath of fresh God.

Ways to Read

A Breath of Fresh God

I hope that *A Breath of Fresh God* serves as both an encouragement to those who seek to follow Christ more closely and as a tool for increasing our sensitivity to recognize Him in unexpected places. Toward that end, it is designed to be read in several different ways.

As a simple, uplifting read:

The easiest and most obvious way to enjoy *A Breath of Fresh God* is just to read it, and to let God touch you through its words and images in whatever way He chooses. I pray that each piece will provide a unique blessing—and a breath.

As a spiritual collaboration:

A Breath of Fresh God is also designed to become not only my book, but yours as well—a collaboration between you (the reader), me (the writer) and God, who is speaking to us both continually. Readings, including Scripture, have the most profound impact on us when we respond to them personally, allowing what was written to open the way for us to explore our own ideas, thoughts, and beliefs more clearly and intricately. Through our own responses, we sometimes find out what we didn't know we knew, and we discover hidden treasures we hadn't recognized in the text during our initial reading.

My own method for Bible study includes copying a passage of Scripture word-for-word; I often see things in the writing that I didn't notice in the reading. Then I turn my notebook on its side so that I can write my own response diagonally across the page (so that my words are different from God's Word). Sometimes I ask questions; other times I imagine what the biblical characters might have been thinking or feeling; sometimes I pick a phrase that stands out and explore it from all angles or apply it to what is currently happening in my life; occasionally, I argue with God (somehow, He always wins those arguments). In the process, I often find that I have learned something from my own writing.

Following each poem, essay, or story in this book is a blank page and an invitation to respond in any way you feel led. This may take the form of paragraphs, bullet points, or a few single, but meaningful words. It could be a sketch, a cartoon, or an abstract drawing that expresses your feelings about what you've read. Maybe you will choose to write a poem or a prayer or even compose a song. Try expressing your thoughts in a variety of different ways.

Now, I confess to being an English teacher who has given essay assignments to many students, but I hope that none of my readers will see these as writing assignments; they are only invitations to explore what the thoughts and questions I have shared from my mind and heart bring up in your own. If nothing comes to mind, just turn the page.

As a devotional study or small group exploration:

"Two heads," they say, "are better than one," and two hearts most certainly are. Reading a book with a group of friends or a study group allows us to share insights and deepen our understanding by considering not only our own impressions, but those of others as well. The "Questions and Activities" section at the back of *A Breath of Fresh God* pairs each piece with questions, exercises, and projects designed to facilitate deeper spiritual consideration, discussion, or exploration.

As an occasional breath:

Among the millions of hats that God wears is that of the Great Archivist who constantly collects, curates, and coordinates our access to the vast sum of human and celestial knowledge. This book may sit on a shelf, like many of our books do, either after we have read them or before we get around to them. These archived texts wait patiently, each bearing its own layer of gathering dust, until the moment when God points it out by bringing it to mind or drops it off the shelf at our feet. He knows just which volume contains the fresh breath of Him that we need. *A Breath of Fresh God* may simply adorn a bookshelf until you occasionally pick it up to see what God has set aside for you for today.

I pray that whichever way you choose to read this book, God will appear to you in some unique way to draw you closer, and that you will catch your breath in pleasant surprise to notice Him once again hanging out nearby.

Take a breath . . .

I sit quietly reading my Bible in the calm of the morning...until, I discover something remarkable in a passage that I've not only read before but know well. I sit up a little taller and read it again more closely.

All at once, I am reminded that I am not just a woman sitting peacefully alone with a bit of leather and a few leaves of paper in my lap. I catch my breath and realize all over again that the One whose saga I'm reading is not an imaginary character in some novel, but the Creator of all the universe, the Master of all I've ever known, the Illustrator behind every picture I've ever seen, and the ultimate Designer of every gadget or tool I've ever used.

And...He is sitting right here next to me.

Abba

I go looking for God
calling out, "Come, Lord,"
and a voice answers:
"I Am here."
I turn toward the sound
and find Him enthroned,
encompassing the stars,
which are the work of His fingers,
yet mysteriously encompassed by them
as they encircle His shoulders
like glittering, celestial fireflies.
He sits above all
looking over all
illumined by a light
beyond the sun.
He reaches out a colossal hand to me.
I squeal, "Abba!"
His great face beams with delight
as He stoops to greet me.
Laughing, I run up to His knees;
laughing, He receives my tiny embrace.
He lifts me into His lap
and lets me play
with the diamonds and sapphires
that adorn his fingers.
His stars twinkle above us,
winking at each other
as I grow tired and lay my head
in the gentle hand
of the King of all creation,
My Daddy.

See Questions and Activities, page 207.

Your Turn

Ask a question, record a thought, sketch a picture, compose a song, make an argument, draw a cartoon, pen a poem, or write a prayer.

If nothing comes to mind, just turn the page.

The Augustinian Ant

When we pass by something, failing to see it because it is so small that it has slipped our notice, we say that we have "overlooked" it. If, on the other hand, we pass by something, failing to see it because it so completely fills our field of vision that it is without edges or parameters, could we say that we have "underlooked" it? I fear that, often, this is how we see, or fail to see, God. If He is indeed everywhere, then He is here, now, watching as we scurry around like unending lines of sugar ants, dutifully taking care of all the important and not-so-important details of our lives.

Or is He?

If I can pass through whole days without noticing Him, how can I know that He is here at all? Perhaps I *am* just a sugar ant, among many other sugar ants, busying myself with tasks that have little significance beyond the meaning I give them during my own short life. How can I know He is really listening when I pray?

Certainly, I'm not the first to puzzle over such a question. Great thinkers like Thomas Aquinas, Anselm of Canterbury, Blaise Pascal, and William Paley have struggled in trying to demonstrate God's Presence. St. Augustine, who had great faith that God was with him, wrestled with many words in his attempts to understand and explain the God in whom he so passionately believed.

Their struggles in confirming God's existence should come as no surprise. Indeed, if God is as resplendent, as invincible, as omniscient, as pervasive as Christians believe, human intellectual tools and perceptions are wholly insufficient for the task of perceiving, much less proving Him. Even an intellect like Augustine's would be like the sugar ant who, in the course of its daily routine of carrying supplies back to its nest, bumps up against the toe of a man standing in its path. The miniscule creature cranes its neck (if indeed, ants have necks) and strains its eyes toward great heights to catch a glimpse of the titanic human toenail.

If that ant, with no more than its ground-level perspective and limited experience, were to attempt to convince the other ants that this toenail they could barely see when the light was just right, was but the smallest appendage of a colossal and sentient being whose loftiness reached into the heavens, which of them would believe him?

If, however, this Augustinian ant was returning from the long and arduous climb up a nearby tree on which he had ascended to great height and looked this mythical human creature in the eye, perhaps his awe-filled account describing its sheer size and beauty and wisdom would prove more persuasive.

If, in fact, many ants had taken such a journey in search of the human-beyond-the-toenail and returned with similar stories of its astounding Presence, would their combined testimony convince their fellows to at least consider the possibility that this mystical being did truly exist?

I can no more prove God than Augustine or Anselm could, but I can add my voice to theirs and join those who have told this legendary story for millennia, describing the God-beyond-the-toenail into whose eyes we have peered, whose voice we have heard, and whose touch we have felt.

But the Being we describe is not only a distant and colossal Presence. Though He is every bit as comparatively large and indescribable as the owner of the toenail our Augustinian ant encountered, He is also nearby and familiar—as close as my next thought. If I am standing before my classroom teaching, He is listening among my students; if I am writing on my computer, He is proofreading the text with me; if I am having coffee with a friend, He laughs at my silly puns; if I am doing laundry or washing dishes, He is sharing in my chores.

Most of the time, I am busy thinking about my daily responsibilities and the common minutiae of my life, and I don't notice that He is hanging around. He is so big and so constantly present that He continues to slip my notice, but that doesn't mean He isn't there; only that I have *underlooked* Him.

See Questions and Activities, page 208.

Your Turn

Ask a question, record a thought, sketch a picture, compose a song, make an argument, draw a cartoon, pen a poem, or write a prayer.

If nothing comes to mind, just turn the page.

Distracted

I am struggling to concentrate,
      to settle down and pray—
            even to identify You
                  in the chaos around me.
I am surrounded by the new,
      by the maybe-this-*should*-be-familiar,
            by the I've-done-this-before-but-not-like-this,
                  by the I'm-not-sure-I-want-to-do-this-again.
My focus is scattered,
      my attention sidetracked,
            my loyalties divided;
                  it is hard to find You—
and then to hold on to the finding.
      Please remind me that
            even when my mind is distracted from You,
                Yours is not distracted from me.
I am sorry when I miss your cues,
      Your gentle nudges,
            Your signs and maps
                showing me which way to turn.
Mark on my calendar the Divine appointments
      you have set for me;
            show me the way
                so that I may arrive on Your time.
Open my eyes to appreciate the wonders
      with which You have surrounded me;
            and let Your Shekinah glisten around me,
                even when I fail to notice it.

See Questions and Activities, page 209.

Your Turn

Ask a question, record a thought, sketch a picture, compose a song, make an argument, draw a cartoon, pen a poem, or write a prayer.

If nothing comes to mind, just turn the page.

And another . . .

I drive to work in the blowing snow, silently willing the stop light to stay green since I'm a few minutes (Okay, maybe more than a few minutes) later than I should be. I chide myself again—if I had just taken the road conditions into account and left a little earlier . . . Intently, I grip the steering wheel and peer through the swirling flakes. Only a few more miles to go.

Then suddenly, my stressing is interrupted. I take a breath and smile as I recall the astonished comment a student made yesterday when she suddenly got it—when what I had been trying to show her for days finally made sense. My fingers on the wheel relax as I remember for whom I work and why I am braving the traffic and the weather to get to work instead of staying by the fire in my nice warm house.

Before the King

I have come here to pray before the High King of heaven. Panting from the exertion of climbing the steep stairs past flocks of huddled and dripping pigeons, I reach the immense front door and step out of the pouring rain into the foyer of His great cathedral. I gaze about in deep awe. Paneled in rich, dark wood with creamy marble floors, this elegant narthex is stunning in every detail. I pause to breathe, listening to the quiet trickle of the ivy-covered fountain recessed into the side wall.

As my eyes grow accustomed to the soft interior light, I make out two maple doors across from where I have entered—great slabs of wood inlaid with delicate images from the life of Christ. They stand at attention, guarding the passage into His sanctuary. My tiptoed steps echo a bit as I cross the marble toward them. The doors are heavy, extending three times my height, but perfectly balanced. I pull one of them open just a crack, enough to peer inside.

I stop short in wonder.

The sanctuary stretches the length of an airplane runway before me. The walls are paneled in the same rich wood, but the floors inside blaze with colors from a luminous marble pavement carefully arranged in elaborate mosaics. Shimmering stained glass windows run up each wall, and pillars soar to great heights, drawing my eyes into the ethereal. At the front of the cathedral, broad marble steps trimmed in gold lead up to an enormous throne where sits... my King.

He is dressed in silks the colors of jewels, and around His shoulders hangs a radiant cape embroidered with gold and copper thread unlike any fabric I've ever seen. It spills down the steps and fills the sanctuary like a billowing sail. Behind Him, the golden pipes of an extraordinary organ ascend toward the lofty ceiling. The King sits surrounded by angels and apostles, as well as those who have kept the faith and honored Him with their lives. His Son stands by His side. I recognize Him: my Lord and my Friend. His robe, seamless and made from the softest wool, also glows with power and warmth. The King and His Son converse quietly.

Though I try to remain unobtrusive, the King glances my way and notices me peeking through the door. He motions for me to come in. My heart begins to beat faster. This is what I came for—to see Him, to speak with Him— yet now that I'm here, I'm not so sure this was a good idea. How can I face Him? How can I presume to talk to Him?

I am not among those who have kept the faith. Often, I have turned aside, distracted by a myriad of earthly inventions. Because I have been concerned with myself, I have missed opportunities to listen to the cares of others. I have been defensive, sometimes striking out in anger or fear. I have forgotten to ask His advice and His direction, deteminedly setting out on my own paths, then being surprised when they come to dead ends. I have known about Him, wondered at Him, worshiped Him…but not always followed. Now that I'm here, what can I say to Him?

Again, He beckons me to come in.

I look down at my ragged skirt. My blouse is in tatters with a coffee stain down the front. I fiddle with a glove I found lying in the street outside. My dripping shoes are rapidly causing a shallow pool to form on the marble at my feet. This is the best I have, but I am certainly not dressed for an audience with the King. Perhaps I should change my mind. I consider turning to flee, but He beckons me a third time. Slowly, I slip through the narrow opening and turn toward the throne. Awkwardly, I walk down the center aisle. Silently, a million—no, more than a million—countless eyes watch my quiet progress.

I stop at the bottom of the steps, unable to move closer. I do not belong here, and yet here I stand, looking up into the face of the King. Out there in the street, I felt confident and strong. I held my head up, ready to face with pride whatever came, but here I am undone. In the light of His glory, I view myself more truly. My inadequacies are obvious for all to see. I've come empty-handed, with nothing to offer my King.

This cannot end well.

I cannot speak. I have no words to express my sorrow. Melting into a puddle of tears, I fall to my knees, keeping my eyes on the cold stones before me. Suddenly, I am immersed in warmth. It flows over me, through me. Pouring over my matted hair and engulfing my tired body, it splashes onto the floor around me. It leaves me clean and refreshed. My ashen hair turns blonde again. The filth is gone from my skin. Even my fingernails are no longer grimy. I look up.

My Lord stands by my side with a dove cooing quietly on His shoulder.

I am left kneeling, unclad before Him, my ragged clothes having been washed away in the deluge. I am clean, but naked and poor in spirit.[1] Those rags were all I had; I have no virtue of my own with which to cover myself.

I still have nothing to offer Him.

But He does not leave me exposed for long. In an instant, my Lord leans down and sweeps His robe around my shoulders. I am completely covered. It feels soft and clean and warm—comfortable—as if this is what I was always meant to wear. My face shines above the soft wool as I look up once again into the eyes of the King. He smiles, no longer seeing the shamed and tattered girl who slipped through the door into His chamber, but rather, one He loves, richly arrayed in the finery of His Son and joyfully bearing His own image. Jesus takes my elbow and gently helps me to stand.

"Welcome, my child," the King says. "You've come home. Come. Sit with me."

With His arm around my shoulder, my Lord escorts me up the steps and, with a smile, presents me to His Father. The King looks deeply into my soul and delights in the Truth He placed in my inward being.[2]

"Sit down with me," the King repeats. "We have much to say to each other." And He begins to teach His wisdom to my secret heart.[2]

NOTES:
[1]Matthew 5:3.
[2]Psalm 51:6.

See Questions and Activities, page 210.

Your Turn

*Ask a question, record a thought, sketch a picture, compose a song,
make an argument, draw a cartoon, pen a poem, or write a prayer.*

If nothing comes to mind, just turn the page.

Rivers of Living Water

*On the last day of the feast, the great day, Jesus
stood up and cried out, "If anyone thirsts, let him
come to me and drink. Whoever believes in me,
as the Scripture has said, 'Out of his heart will
flow rivers of living water.'"*
                                                    —John 7:37–38

"Rivers of Living Water…"
    organic tributaries
        gracefully surging forward
            in deliberate progress.
                Incarnate water; Spirit rivers
                    flowing from those who believe.

But what does Living Water look like, feel like?
    Does it ebb and flow around us?
        Does it rush like a fierce flood,
            or imperceptibly rise around our toes
                and up to our knees?
                    Does it feel cold as it reaches our bellies?

And how can I open the floodgates
    to let those rivers stream through me,
        out of me, into the hearts
            of the people whose lives I share:
                both those who thrill at Christ's touch
                    and those who can't yet fathom Him?

Lord, I have seen Your Shekinah—
    Your light shining in the darkness.
        I have felt Your Spirit, Your Pentecostal fire
            warming my heart at unexpected moments,
                exciting my mind
                    with unimagined possibilities.

But if I gaze on Your Light,
    then turn from its brightness,
        returning to the work of my day,
            the Light seems to fade,
                and I find myself again
                    in the darkening shadows.

After I thrill in the exhilaration of your Fire,
    I get up from my knees
        to face daily frustrations
            as the warmth in my heart cools,
                and my excitement dulls
                    into the ordinary.

But how shall I stand in the deluge
    of an abiding,
        life-enhancing river—
            a torrent, not my own,
                but flowing from deep inside my own soul
                    more tangible than light and fire?

A Breath of Fresh God

If I am inundated
    in Your living, surging, refreshing current
        rising to my knees, my waist, my chest, my chin
            and washing over me in waves
                until I emerge drenched
                    and breathless,

then even when I turn back
    to common tasks,
        I am still wet,
            dripping with Your Spirit
                and leaving a puddle around my toes
                    wherever I stand.

I quiver in the Sonlight,
    shaking droplets from my hair and my clothes
        all over the people around me
            like an over-exuberant puppy,
                surprising them,
                    and making them a little bit wet too.

Lord, I am, indeed, thirsty for this Living Water.
    Come, drench me in Your River.
        Flow into me, through me, out of me,
            and teach me to offer a taste of Your Spirit Drink
                to all the people I encounter.
                    They, too, are thirsty.

See Questions and Activities, page 211.

Your Turn

Ask a question, record a thought, sketch a picture, compose a song, make an argument, draw a cartoon, pen a poem, or write a prayer.

If nothing comes to mind, just turn the page.

The Gallery

My husband, David, and I weren't ready to "settle down" when we got married, so we sold most of what we owned, put the rest into storage, and took up residence in my aging Datsun. We were just a couple of kids setting off on a grand adventure together. We didn't know that we were embarking on a tour of the greatest Museum of Fine Arts ever collected. We saw no Picassos or Rembrandts or da Vincis. Instead, we discovered the glorious works of the Great Master Himself.

During the next three and a half months, we covered 16,000 miles of highway (plus a few dirt roads) from Florida to Canada, from the Atlantic to the Pacific. "Home" was anywhere we pitched the heavy, old-fashioned, canvas elk-hunting tent that we carried on top of the Datsun. My dog, a husky-timber wolf cross named Pasquinel, shared the backseat with our ice cooler.

As we set off across the United States, we noticed the masterpieces beginning to appear. Each turn in the road brought before us another magnificent work of art. It began with a lovely watercolor—a beach scene from the gulf coast of Florida. We stepped across the concrete sidewalk which framed the piece onto a stippled white beach. The sand was so fine that it coated our bare feet like sugar on a donut. A calm green sea lounged in the background, rising and falling with each new brush stroke, while baking figures lay on colorful towels, accenting the brightness of the shoreline. The Artist drew bold arcs across the sky, using swooping seagulls and pelicans as tiny paintbrushes.

Two months later, we viewed a very different seascape. Off the Oregon coast, the waves tumbled down the canvas as if trying to beat each other to the shore. They crashed against darkly shadowed rocks, sending columns of water twenty feet into the air. A wave didn't have time to subside before the Master splashed the white froth of its successor on top of it. The seagulls here seemed to have been drawn in with a pencil; small, lonely Vs against an angry grey sky.

Another painting appeared before us when we camped in the thick forest of the Ozark Mountains near Arkansas' Buffalo River. In the charcoal air of growing dusk, hundreds of shades of green blended, twisting around and through each other yet remaining distinct. In contrast to the deep greens of the woods around us, a stark white cliff rose out of the murky river in the background. The colors were deep and rich, as if the paint was still wet; as if only a few minutes before the Artist had stood there adding the final details to His canvas.

We headed west and hiked upward to 12,000 feet in Wyoming's Snowy Range, where we discovered that the

Master is also a skillful jeweler. There, He had carefully set a high-country gem among the tiny wildflowers between the silver prongs of barren peaks. The surface of that timber-line lake had been cut and polished with such precision that it reflected colored rays of light back into the face of the bright afternoon sun. Such a jewel could be worn only on the hand of Lady Earth whom He created.

Later, at Craters of the Moon National Monument in Idaho, we found the volcanic remains of God's artwork from many years ago. We descended into a dark cave where lava once flowed like a steaming subterranean river. Now the temperature inside the cave never rises above freezing. The beam from our flashlight revealed a curtain of frozen lace crocheted across the black wall where water has been slowly dripping for centuries. That night, our tent stood on a mound of crushed lava. The light from our cooking fire choreographed strange, dancing shadows across the volcanic sculptures that surrounded us. For a moment, I wondered if our flame might reignite the long-dead fires inside those rocks.

A more recent piece of the Master's volcanic artwork awaited us in Washington State. Some years before, He must have looked back at the long-completed work of Mt. St. Helens with its perfect, snowcapped cone and decided it was time for a revision. It took Him only a few seconds to rearrange millions of tons of rock and earth into a new shape, centered around a deep, smoldering crater. Today, the mountain stands 1,300 feet shorter than it did before.

As a sculptor, the Master has achieved a level of accomplishment of which human artists can only dream. His statues don't stand still like the ones we see in city parks and on courthouse lawns. God's sculptures walk and fly and eat. One, a giant bull elk, joined us for brunch in Canada's Banff National Park. His great rack seemed cast in bronze, stretching four feet from point to point. The morning sunlight shone across the powerful muscles of his shoulders as he walked through the brush behind our tent. Pasquinel barked and strained at her leash, but the bull only lifted his regal head and stared at us with dark, liquid eyes. Then he went back to chewing leaves. We watched in respectful awe until he finished his breakfast and disappeared into the trees.

Further north, in Jasper National Park, we found the Master working in a different medium: ice sculpture. God's work on the Athabasca Glacier which spills off the heights of the one hundred and twenty-five square-mile Columbia Icefield began millennia ago during the last ice age. It continues each day as He builds on here and cuts away there. The ice serves as both His artistic medium and His sculpting tool. He uses the ice to carve the surrounding stones, while at the same time, the contour of the glacial flow is molded by the rocks and peaks that rise around it. Leftover scraps from His work gradually melt and flow into brilliant turquoise lakes that glow like stained glass windows on a sunny day.

Mental photographs of these works of art still hang in my memory, though we have long-since settled down. We now live inside of a beautiful oil painting—a landscape depicting a quiet Colorado mountain valley. The Master constantly revises the picture, adding gold to the trees in the fall and covering the landscape in white each winter. He often lets us watch while He splashes pastel pinks and corals across the ice-blue sky around a disappearing gold-ringed sun. If I look, I can see His signature among the clouds.

Watching the Master at work reminds me that He has commissioned us as the curators of His Great Global Gallery. In His honor, it is our job to care for these paintings and look after these statues. We are cast as both admirers and caretakers of this world which He is constantly recreating.[1]

NOTES:

[1] A previous version of "The Gallery" was originally published as "Artwork by the Great Master" in *Seek* magazine by the Standard Publishing Company, Cincinnati, OH, February, 1991.

See Questions and Activities, page 213.

Your Turn

Ask a question, record a thought, sketch a picture, compose a song, make an argument, draw a cartoon, pen a poem, or write a prayer.

If nothing comes to mind, just turn the page.

A stirring . . .

Taking a break from my duties at home, I step out to go for a walk. It is a pleasant spring day. My mind wanders through whatever thoughts have taken my fancy for the moment. My eye traces the lazy shadows of the pine trees that the afternoon sun has painted across the road. The birds twitter, and the squirrels chatter.

All at once, the whole scene comes into sharper focus. The sky becomes a brighter blue, and the trees take on more vibrant and varied shades of green. The individual needles in the tops of the pines become distinct. I recognize not only the general twitter of many birds, but the particular calls of three or four different varieties, and I pick out the tap-tap-tap of a woodpecker hammering the trunk of a far-off tree. Everything seems unexpectedly clearer. It is as if the creation all around me has suddenly become acutely aware of the Creator passing by. The natural world stands at attention in His Presence which is reflected in all He has created, myself included.

Eight Billion Pixels

Genesis tells us that we are all made in the image of God.[1] But what does that mean?

We reason that if we display His image, God must somehow be similar to us. We use what we see in ourselves and in the people around us to devise a list of characteristics from which we attempt to describe God in a sort of spiritual reverse engineering. Although we recognize that He is Spirit, in our minds and our descriptions of Him, we endow Him with arms and legs like ours, with a heart that beats in love like ours, with thoughts and emotions like ours. We know the Scripture: "For my thoughts are not your thoughts, neither are your ways my ways, declares the Lord. For as the heavens are higher than the earth, so are my ways higher than your ways and my thoughts than your thoughts."[2] Still, since we bear His image, we imagine Him to be like us.

This assumption is actually backwards: if we bear His image, it is we who must somehow resemble Him—not the other way around. How, then, can we, with our mortal limits, mirror an infinite God? Saint Augustine asks, "Is there, indeed, O Lord my God, aught in me that can contain Thee?"[3] Yet, what other clues do we have about who God is and what He is like besides what we can see in His image bearers all around us?

Perhaps our difficulty stems from our individualistic idea of what it means to bear His image. When Genesis says, "So God created man in his own image, in the image of God he created him; male and female he created them,"[4] we usually interpret that to mean that each of us exhibits the likeness of this Immortal, Almighty, Omniscient God—a whole picture of Him. Yet, every time we look around and see Jaylin or Jace or Joy or Josiah or Jada or Jenna, we know that we are not looking at an ideal portrayal of God. Even if we love them dearly, we still notice that they sometimes fray a little about the edges. They exhibit occasional flaws and gaps and inconsistencies that just can't be accurate illustrations of our perfect God. When we look deeply into ourselves, we become even more convinced that what we see cannot exemplify the Divine.

Perhaps instead, our image-bearing is a collective act.

None of us could begin to reflect an image that could be an accurate picture, or even rough approximation, of the whole character of God. Instead, we each carry what we can: a tiny piece—a pixel in the vast picture of a God who is so immense and magnificent that to mirror Him requires every one of the nearly eight billion people with whom we share Earth, plus all those who have lived before us and all who will follow. Though God is complete in Himself, the *image* of Him that we are created to display becomes sharper and more detailed each time another pixel-bearer is added to the picture.

God told Abraham, "Look toward heaven, and number the stars, if you are able to number them…So shall your offspring be,"[5] When Abraham looked up as God had directed him, he was impressed. It was not any single star, but rather the countless, cosmic whole that made him catch his breath in wonder at God's promise.

I once attended a church conference where the backdrop for the proceedings was an enormous mosaic made up of small, individual photos. From close up, it looked like a multitude of human faces, but from the back of the room, the shades and contrasts of these little pictures formed a massive mural depicting the face of Christ.

Every one of us displays a tiny piece of God's image—a unique pixel that reflects a speck of light which contributes to our vast vision of the God we serve. He didn't create me in His image; He created *us* in His image.

Of course, each of us can decide whether to hold up our little pixel to reflect His light or to sit on it and keep it hidden. If we don't choose to show the part of God which we were uniquely made to display, then our section of His likeness is darkened a little. That tiny hole does nothing to dim the character of God Himself; it only limits our shared ability to see Him clearly. If we become selfish, focusing not on our contribution to the whole picture, but on an over-importance of our one little part, the likeness becomes pixelated and difficult to discern.

On the other hand, if all of us lift our own pixels high

so that they can reflect the brilliance of God in concert, we participate in enlightening everyone. His appearance becomes rich, vibrant, and distinct as we reveal the intricate elements of His character for one another. His essence flows and moves through and around us. It is then that we, together, truly bear the image of God.

NOTES:
[1] Genesis 1:27.
[2] Isaiah 55: 8–9.
[3] Saint Augustine, *The Confessions of Saint Augustine*, AD 401. Translated by E. B. Pusey (Edward Bouverie), Project Gutenberg. https://www.gutenberg.org/files/3296/3296-h/3296-h.htm.
[4] Genesis 1:27.
[5] Genesis 15:5.

See Questions and Activities, page 214.

Your Turn

*Ask a question, record a thought, sketch a picture, compose a song,
make an argument, draw a cartoon, pen a poem, or write a prayer.*

If nothing comes to mind, just turn the page.

Letters from Abroad

I t took me fifty-four years to get across the Atlantic.

As a kid, I took a book nearly everywhere I went so that whenever I had to ride a bus or stand in line, I could mentally disappear into someplace I'd never seen before. I fell in love with Russia when I was ten and later studied Soviet politics and Russian in college. I browsed the study abroad ads wistfully, but never had the money to go. Later, as a homeschool mom, I dreamed of taking my children on a grand field trip to _____ (fill in the blank with whichever country we were reading about). Many times, I imagined this trip or that one, but each time I figured up the costs and multiplied by six, my plans dissolved into fantasy.

When our last child was approaching graduation from our homeschool, I teased my husband that twenty-two years of homeschooling should be enough to earn a retirement.

He just as teasingly offered me a "generous percentage" of what I'd been making. Though he couldn't offer me a paycheck, he started saving money for the international trip I'd never been able to take.

Two years later, we flew to Ireland. We spent two stunning weeks in the British Isles before he had to return home to work. For me, God had arranged another opportunity to dovetail with our travel plans—I went on to Prague and Slovakia for a week on my own and a visit with an old friend. Then I met up with an American teaching team and continued on to East Kazakhstan, where we served as guest instructors at the Kazakh American Free University.

Traveling abroad was like watching the words from the books I'd read rise off the page to become 3D before my eyes. Histories, biographies, stories from classic literature, and odd facts that I'd known for years took on new depth, new meaning, new importance when viewed in local rather than historical context. I saw the fingerprints of God on everything, old and new, and I discovered "a-ha" moments around the corners of every thirteenth century cathedral and each convoluted train station.

Attempting to reverse the process of words transforming themselves into 3D materialities, I tried to translate my amazement back into words in a series of letters to the people I'd left at home. In the European museums I visited, I found faded and water-marked letters that had traveled many miles and survived centuries before finding their places behind the display glass. In contrast, my missives were instantly absorbed into "the cloud" and delivered with electronic immediacy, carrying my observations across the globe for the entertainment of my friends on the American side of the Atlantic.

On Irish Cathedrals

A very wet greeting to you from the west coast of Scotland! Thank you all for your email notes and your prayers.

David and I have been winding our way through the Irish countryside on very narrow roads (on the left side—which is harder than it sounds, especially when driving "backwards" around roundabouts!). Buildings that date from the twelfth century abound: castles and cathedrals with intricate stone carvings, one-hundred-foot towers, elaborate pipe organs, tightly-pieced stained glass, massive pillars reaching up toward soaring ceilings, and nine-hundred-year-old cornerstones.

I am constantly reminded of an old story about the construction of a medieval cathedral . . .

A curious visitor came onto the building site to find a blacksmith twisting the bars of a huge iron gate.

"What are you doing?" the visitor asked. The blacksmith explained the process of heating metal and then carefully hammering it into place. The vistor thanked him and went on toward the unfinished building where a stone mason sat tapping the edge of a square block of granite.

"What are you doing?" he asked the workman. The mason responded by giving him a quick lesson in the art of fitting one stone to another. A little farther inside the visitor discovered a wood carver putting the finishing touches on a detailed relief of Jesus as the Good Shepherd.

"What are you doing?" he repeated. The woodcutter just grunted, not interested in interruptions.

Finally, as the sightseer turned to leave, he met an old woman carefully sweeping up after the artisans.

"And what are you doing?" he asked her. She stopped

sweeping, leaned on her broom, and looked up into the face of Jesus in the colored glass above her head.

"I am building a cathedral to the glory of almighty God!"[1]

As we wander through places where God has been worshiped for almost a thousand years, I hope that my life, like hers, is building a cathedral—a lasting legacy that will remind people of Christ and draw their eyes and hearts up to Him for many years to come.

Before we got to western Ireland, David and I had commented to each other that no modern congregation would take the time or effort to build such elaborate houses of worship as these medieval edifices; even if they wanted to, such a project would be prohibitively expensive now. Then in Galway, we found a cathedral that was every bit as awe-inspiring as its ancient predecessors, but which had been completed in 1965. I am older than it is! It seems that taking on big projects for God may not be as impossible or cost prohibitive as we might imagine.

This morning, we attended church in Belfast twice— first in a Catholic church and then in a Protestant one. For me, that felt symbolic, given the violence and divisiveness I remember from news reports when I was a teenager. Then we took a blustery two-hour ferry ride to Scotland, changing countries (well, sort of—technically Northern Ireland and Scotland are both part of Britain).

Not all of our visits have been to churches. The other night I got to present one of my poems to a group of Irish poets who meet to share their work each week in a local pub in the city of Limerick. The Irish are known for their poetry, and getting to join them as a guest (they introduced me simply as "Charissa from Colorado") was a special treat.

One final bit of trivia: the Irish don't only drive on the left; they walk on the left as well. I kept running into people when I met them on the sidewalk because, like most Americans, I stepped to the right.

May you all be blessed.

In Christ's Peace,
Charissa

A Literary Week

Last week was a literary week. On Thursday we spent five hours in Westminster Cathedral visiting the resting places of historical figures like Queen Elizabeth and Mary Queen of Scots (buried across the hall from each other, despite the fact that Elizabeth ordered Mary's beheading). Wandering among the memorials to Charles Dickens, Geoffrey Chaucer, and C.S. Lewis in Poet's Corner was almost like meeting my favorite literary geniuses. In the evening we watched debates in both the House of Lords and in the House of Commons, where two-hundred years ago, William Wilberforce presented his bill to abolish the slave trade year after year until it finally passed.

The next day it was on to Canterbury Cathedral, seat of the Archbishop of Canterbury, site of the martyrdom of Thomas a Becket, and famous destination of Chaucer's tale-telling pilgrims (I tortured many students with *Murder in the Cathedral* and *Canterbury Tales*). I, too, was a pilgrim there.

Then Saturday, we took the train north to Stratford-upon-Avon, hometown of William Shakespeare (I guess I have inflicted one or two of his plays on students as well). Surrounded by phrases from familiar dramas, we walked through a village that is truly a marriage between the sixteenth century and the twenty-first. We enjoyed *Cymbeline*, a play that is all-Shakespeare with a hundred twists and turns of plot, betrayals, misunderstandings, and even a happy ending (despite it having been originally listed as a "tragedie" in the first published version of Shakespeare's plays).[2] Then Sunday morning we attended services in the church where the Bard is buried.

Each of these famous names belongs to a person who made a unique contribution to culture for which he or she is remembered and known, but surrounding each of them in the churches and cemeteries where they are buried, are thousands of others whose names I didn't recognize; people who no one living cares to remember. Some of their gravestones have even become too weathered to read. They, too, made unique contributions to their families, their cities, their churches, and the lives of those around them. I am reminded that I don't remember them, but God does.

I realized as we rode the train to Canterbury that, in the unfamiliarity of a different country every few days and the unsettledness of being perpetually lost, I have forgotten to pray for the people around me. When we lived in Philadelphia, I had a standard practice of getting on a subway and then praying one-by-one for each of the people with whom I shared the car—but that was on a familiar train to known places. There I knew where to get on and off. Here I've been somewhat anxious—are we on the right train? Which stop is ours? Have I forgotten or failed to understand something critical? Where can I find a bathroom?

It is easy to forget that everyone else on the train has

their own struggles and anxieties and their own forms of lostness. So, today, I am trying to begin again in remembering to pray not only for my own journey, but also for theirs, as they each live and work, making impacts that will be remembered or forgotten by those to come, but certainly remembered by God.

Yesterday David flew west and I flew east.

He is home today, and I am in Prague.

In Christ's Peace,
Charissa

Lost Language

Hello! And blessings to you all.

Last week I landed in Prague and lost my words. As a writer and speaker and teacher, I am very dependent on language, but last week I spent two days largely alone in Prague where I couldn't read the signs or understand the people speaking around me. I was staying with a missionary family, which was helpful in the evenings when I could pelt them with questions, but in the daytimes, I was quite alone in a city full of people talking to one another. There truly was a language barrier, and it felt very isolating. I learned to listen for clues and puzzle out signs, making assumptions about words that held bits of English or Latin or Russian roots that I could recognize.

Prague is a stunningly beautiful city, so I took myself on a "squirrel tour," walking in one direction until something interesting caught my eye (which usually took less than a block) and then turning to investigate. My path was definitely not a straight line. Thanks to the GPS on my phone and a three-day subway pass, I was sure I could get back to where I was staying—until I got myself so lost that even GPS couldn't unravel it. I tried to ask for help, but I couldn't make people understand my questions, nor did I have any hope of understanding their rapidly-spoken answers. After two hours of trying to find my way on my own, I was very grateful when I discovered someone who spoke English. It was humbling to recognize that she was doing me a great favor in choosing to speak my language because I couldn't speak hers.

Perhaps that same barrier exists between us and God. Human beings don't naturally speak His language, though I think we all want to on some level, just as I wanted to speak to the Czechs around me in Prague. We are lost and frustrated without His answers to our questions. To be alone in the world is scary, but just as I couldn't suddenly learn Czech, we can't suddenly learn God's language either. It takes years of studying, doing lessons in His Book, and spending time practicing in conversations with Him. Thankfully, in the meantime, He does speak my language and chooses often to switch out of His more beautiful and expressive native tongue to communicate with me in the courser ways that I can comprehend.

In Prague I started even the simplest inquiry with, "Do you speak English?"

The answer was often, "A little."

Perhaps in my study of God's language, I am far enough along to be able to answer the same: "I speak it a little." But I know I've yet a long way to go to become fluent.

From Prague, I took a train to Slovakia to visit Ludee, an old friend (actually she is younger than I am, so I should say she is a friend from many years ago). She gave me the gift of companionship—a chance to catch up on our children, to share our hearts, to go on adventures to thirteenth century castles, to run for the last bus (which we almost missed), and to laugh together. She also gave me the gift of her words. For the three days I was with her, she managed where we were going, figured out train and bus schedules, bought the tickets, and translated for me as other people spoke. It was a break from the pressure and exhaustion of trying to figure it all out without my words. When she took me to the bus to leave for Germany, she even spoke to the driver and asked him to make announcements in English as well as Slovakian so I could understand. Unfortunately, he promptly forgot her request.

Today, that bus dropped me off on the street in Frankfurt, where, once again, I understood nothing, but I must be getting better at this. I found the train station, came up with the right change for a ticket, and arrived at my hotel. It wasn't even scary this time. Now, I'm off again, not only to a new country but a new continent; I meet my team and fly to Kazakhstan tomorrow.

May God continue to be with each one of you in your studies, as your vocabulary in His language grows.

In Christ's Peace,
Charissa

Dasha

The Spirit of God is uninhibited by language barriers. Despite the service being entirely in Russian, His Presence in the church we attended this morning was clearly communicated. It was a joy-filled gathering of brothers and sisters from a variety of nationalities. After teaching twenty hours of classes in the past four days with people speaking in unfamiliar words all around me, I'd become frustrated with trying to decipher the Russian and had started depending on translation whenever it was available. I could pick out a few words here and there, but most of them didn't even land as they flew by in rapid dialogue.

I discovered when the singing began with the words projected onto a screen, that I could understand far more than I could in general conversation. I could read all of the Cyrillic and understand quite a few of the words, either directly or by context, so I could sing along and really worship. (It made me wish that people could have subtitles printed across their chests as they speak in daily chat). I was thrilled to find I could recognize the Lord's Prayer.

As the sermon began, I knew the pastor would outpace both my ear for Russian and my vocabulary. I prayed for God to open my understanding so that I could get some sense of what he was saying. A minute later, while I was still praying and my eyes were still closed, a soft, sweet voice came into my ear. Dasha, one of my students from last week, had come to sit down next to me and had begun to translate. She spoke quietly in my ear through the entire sermon. I told her afterwards that she had been God's answer to my prayer.

When I had first run into Dasha at church before the service began, I was a little surprised to see her. The church was about four miles across the city from the university, and I saw no other students there. However, when I thought

about it, I didn't know why I had been surprised. Dasha had stood out in class, not because of special ability (although her English is very good), but because she was bright and joyful and curious, a light in the classroom. I had been immediately drawn to her. We had talked after class and agreed to meet for coffee sometime next week. When it turned out that she knows Christ, it made perfect sense: her light had shone at school, and her gift of words was truly a blessing to me at church. I only hope that my own Christ-Light shines as brightly as hers as I go back into classes for another very busy week of teaching.
Blessings to you all.

In Christ's Peace,
Charissa

Fire!

We've just completed another week of teaching. I taught classes in English, political theory, academic writing, and American history (the Russian and Kazakh students were amazingly interested in our history and incredibly well-versed in what is happening in our election.) Somewhere in the middle of this week when, if I wasn't standing in a classroom, I was preparing to teach, I got a 2:00 a.m. text from a friend in Colorado who didn't know I was abroad (it was the middle of the afternoon for her). She said she had heard about "the fire" and wondered if I was okay.

Fire? What fire?

I realized I hadn't heard anything from David in almost forty-eight hours. It was the middle of the next day before I could get onto the internet to find information on what was happening back home in Beulah.

The pictures on the news brought tears—the flames were clearly less than a mile from our house, and I still hadn't heard from David. When he finally did text that evening, he opened with, "I'd hoped you wouldn't hear." He went on to explain that he had evacuated with all of our livestock and was living in the barn at the State Fair Grounds, caring for everyone's evacuated small animals.

About half an hour after I'd seen the news report on the fire, I also heard news about a Category 4 hurricane which had come across Haiti, where the kids I taught last summer live, and was expected to hit South Carolina. My daughter, Aspen, lives in South Carolina.

In many ways this entire Eurasian adventure has been spent watching God arrange things. He has repeatedly solved issues before me as I went. It has been about learning to trust Him when I had no familiarity, no language, and no control over situations. Now David is dealing with a fire evacuation, our house is dangerously close to the flames, and Aspen is about to experience her first hurricane….and here I am in Kazakhstan, precisely halfway (twelve time zones) around the world. I am reminded again that although I am far away, God is with David and his evac-ed menagerie; He will sit with Aspen through the storm; He is watching over our home; and He will board the plane with me tomorrow when I begin the very long trip home (six more sets of take-offs and landings). On both sides of the world, it's still about trusting the One who is really in control.

In Christ's Peace,
Charissa

Walking Among Miracles

Home again.

My trip to Europe and Asia included eight countries, twelve plane rides (not to mention buses, trams, subways, ferry boats, rental cars, trains, and taxis), forty hours of classroom time, and countless miracles.

I cannot number the times when, dropping into a new city and needing to figure out train schedules and street signs, I looked up to find God opening a much-needed door, providing a glimmer of understanding even in a foreign language, or leading a friendly English-speaking native my way. He protected my health when travel started to take its toll; He showed me landmarks when I was lost; and He arranged several divine appointments that I couldn't possibly have booked.

On the seventeen-hour bus ride from Zilina, Slovakia to Frankfurt, Germany, I felt quite isolated and alone, not being able to understand the announcements on the bus or talk to anyone around me. In the middle of the night, a young man who spoke English boarded the bus in Austria and sat next to me. I had been writing in a notebook, and he asked what I was doing. When I said it was a Bible study, he told me that he was also a Christian. He went on to talk about his struggles in starting a new job and finding his place in the world.

On the long plane ride to Kazakhstan, my seat mate was a man who had grown up in Soviet Kazakhstan, but who had made the unusual choice to turn to Christ when he was sixteen. When he was eighteen, he was conscripted into the Soviet army, where he had to withstand daily berating and brain washing as they tried to get him to turn away from his faith. He stood his ground. Years later, as he put it, "God opened the door" for him to take his family of nine children and emigrate to the United States. He is now a pastor in Washington State and was returning to Kazakhstan to see family members. We talked for a long time. He was certainly an encouragement to me (though he told me how bad my Russian was), and I hope that I was able to encourage him as well.

Finally, I met a sweet young woman at the university. She, too, had already discovered the blessing of giving her life to Christ, but was confused by the disparity between what her faith taught her was right and what she saw around her. She sounded discouraged and struggled with how to live out Christ in a culture that often didn't support Christian choices. I got to speak with her briefly several times and then had tea with her on the last night I was in Ust-Komenogorsk. I was blessed to have the opportunity to share in her struggles, to lift her up, and to confirm her choices.

After flying home (through six security/immigration checks), I found two more miracles waiting for me. First, my daughter, Miriam, picked me up from the airport on her way home from Billings, Montana, where she had been visiting her cousin, Sam. We had all been called to his bed-side in July to say goodbye, but God had other plans. His mother had cared for him through August and September as he gradually lost function and very nearly completed the process of dying. Then in late September, a crisis brought a new doctor and a surgery that others had called impossible. Miri visited him in a rehab unit where he was laughing, joking, and learning to walk again. We expected a funeral, but God gave him a new chance at life.

And then there was Beulah, where David had only

recently returned from being evacuated. He had left the valley under a mandatory order, with the heat from the fire and the ashes coming down on his head underscoring his need to leave.

He doubted there would be a house to return to.

Today, I took a long walk around the valley. To the east I could see the charred hillside, but to the west, the gold of the aspens and deep burgundy of the oaks were set against evergreens and blue mountains. The burn mark clearly proved that the fire could have taken my valley, but thanks to the grace of God and the efforts of many expert fire fighters, it didn't.

So I have returned from adventures laced with miracles on the other side of the world to walk again the familiar roads of the stunning little mountain valley I call home. Truly, God's miracles are everywhere.

In Christ's Peace,
Charissa

NOTES:

[1] This is my retelling of a story that has been in my head for a long time. I don't know where it came from, though I suspect that I heard it in a sermon somewhere years ago. Although I cannot name its original writer, I acknowledge a debt of gratitude for a tale that has breathed a bit of God into my heart many times, reminding me of my purpose in whatever current task God has laid before me.

[2] Shakespeare, William, "Cymbeline" (Folio 1, 1623) *Internet Shakespeare Editions, https://internetshakespeare.uvic.ca/doc/Cym_F1/index.html.*

See Questions and Activities, page 215.

Your Turn

Ask a question, record a thought, sketch a picture, compose a song, make an argument, draw a cartoon, pen a poem, or write a prayer.

If nothing comes to mind, just turn the page.

Ты or Вы?

As is done in many languages, Russian uses two
different word forms for what we translate to English
as "you." One is the familiar Ты (tee), which is used for family,
close friends, and people of similar status as ourselves. The
other is the more formal Вы (vwee), which provides an address
for people with whom we aren't on such comfortable terms:
elders, those of greater status, people we don't know well.

Several years ago, when I had the opportunity to teach at
the Kazakh American Free University in Ust-Komenogorsk,
Kazakhstan, I attended church and was surprised to hear God
addressed with the familiar Ты. This was God we were talking
to—the Creator of all the universe; the King whose train filled
the temple of Isaiah's vision;[1] the all-encompassing cloud and
consuming fire who engulfed Mt. Horeb when Moses ascended.[2]

God!

Especially in the formal Kazakh-Russian culture where
honoring a person's status is important, I expected God to be

addressed as Вы. If my boss or a student's professor ranked a formal Вы, shouldn't God? Instead, He was approached with the same language as we would use to speak to a friend or child.

This verbal dilemma leaves me pondering: how should we approach God—as Ты or Вы? Is He King of all the earth or the gentle loving Father into whose lap I crawl? In English, we capitalize words that refer to God, sometimes even including adjectives and pronouns; it is a matter of honor. The ancient Hebrews took this idea of linguistic honor even further, refusing to pronounce the name of God and abbreviating it in written form as YHVH because it was considered too holy for human use. And yet my Russian friends addressed Him in the comfortable Ты? Would we honor Him with a formal equivalent of Вы if English contained such a semantic distinction? Or would our more informal culture also address the Friend and Lover of our souls with the familiar Ты? Who is He really, Ты or Вы?

Though this is a minor linguistic predicament, its implications beg a much bigger question which has perplexed both lofty theologians and common pray-ers since the beginning of theological history: exactly who is God? And who are we in relation to this all-powerful and all-knowing Deity?

Indeed, to live out our Christian faith is to embrace, and even to revel in, several incomprehensible paradoxes—ideas that appear so contradictory that it seems they must be mutually exclusive, but which, as it turns out, exist side by side.

The first of these is the contradiction we find in our own natures. Sometimes, I become intensely aware of being inadequate, insecure, and culpable. I am the worm wearing filthy rags; worthless and drowning in sins of my own choosing. Yet at other times, I am confident and strong. I know beyond any doubt that I am beloved, cherished, and protected; a daughter of the King Himself.

The eighteenth century philosopher Blaise Pascal wrote, "What sort of freak then is man! How novel, how monstrous, how chaotic, how paradoxical, how prodigious! Judge of all things, feeble earthworm, repository of truth, sink of doubt and error, glory and refuse of the universe."[3]

It's no wonder I am confused!

The second paradox is equally hard to get our minds around: that of the incongruity within God's character. On one hand, we are told that God is so far beyond our comprehension that our small intellects can't begin to plumb His depth. Isaiah quotes God saying, "For my thoughts are not your thoughts, neither are your ways my ways, declares the Lord. For as the heavens are higher than the earth, so are my ways higher than your ways and my thoughts than your thoughts."[4] In the New Testament, God's ascendency is described in regard to Jesus, saying, "He is the radiance of the glory of God and the exact imprint of his nature, and he upholds the universe by the word of his power."[5]

We worship the God who made the stars and came up with the intricacies of the human eye; who designed galaxies and holds the nucleus of each tiny atom together with a strong nuclear force that scientists still can't fully define or understand. His thoughts truly are beyond our thoughts and His ways beyond our ways. Yet, at the same time, He is as close as the "pneuma," the breath or spirit within us.[6] He numbers our hairs, and He knows our hearts better than we know them ourselves. He is right here with us—Emmanuel.

The famous prayer, "St. Patrick's Breastplate," puts it like this:

"Christ with me,
Christ before me,

Christ behind me,
Christ in me,
Christ beneath me,
Christ above me,
Christ on my right,
Christ on my left,
Christ when I lie down,
Christ when I sit,
Christ when I arise,
Christ in the heart of everyone who thinks of me,
Christ in the mouth of everyone who speaks of me,
Christ in every eye that sees me,
Christ in every ear that hears me."[7]

God truly is beyond our comprehension…and He is a bit scary. He can look into our thoughts, know our histories, see our motivations, and touch our souls. For the conflicted creature Pascal describes, facing this overwhelmingly awe-inspiring Personage who knows our intimate secrets could indeed be reason to flee as rapidly as possible in the opposite direction (though I'm not sure which way might be the opposite direction from God)—unless somehow, He knows all about us, and (inexplicably) He likes us anyway, indeed, loves us; unless, rather than threatening, He really is inviting us to rest and revel in the love of a gentle Father.

Most Christians understand intellectually that both descriptions of God's character are true, but experientially, we separate them, sometimes thinking of awesome Divinity, and other times cuddling up in His fatherly kindness. How do we learn to experience both God the eminent and God the intimate at the same time? How can we, who are insignificant and flawed, yet beloved and made holy, reverently kneel before the King of kings and Lord of lords, and at the same time trust and cherish the intimate Lover of our souls? How do we get our minds around this dichotomy, which isn't really a dichotomy at all, but a mysterious unity?

So I come back again to my original question: Should I address God as Ты or Вы?

Most other languages that make a distinction between familiar and formal pronouns are in agreement with the Russians. God, it seems, is typically addressed in the friendly and the familiar. English (with its strange penchant for exceptions and for exceptions to its exceptions) has taken the opposite approach—but (of course) with some exceptions.

Most English speakers use only one second-person pronoun: you. We make no division regarding who that "you" might be. The "You" that addresses God, is different only in its capitalization. "You," however, is actually the formal form of the word. Once upon a time, English did make the distinction: "ye" or "you" was the formal pronoun and "thou" or "thy" was used among those who knew each other well. "Thou" sort of fell out of English in the seventeenth and eighteenth centuries, leaving us with no other choice but "you."[8]

Consequently, English speakers seem to run counter to their international brothers and sisters, addressing God in the secretly-formal "You" form. Except (we are, after all, talking about English here) in many church-related contexts like prayer books, hymns, formal services, and the popularly-repeated versions of the Lord's Prayer and the Twenty-third Psalm, that archaic seventeenth-century "thou" still shows up. So, in the end, the only place where we English speakers still regularly use the familiar address is when we approach God. Even we, who are reluctant to make a formal/familiar distinction, speak to God in our nearest equivalent of the Ты.

I'm not looking to argue over semantics with the whole rest of the world, but I am still a little torn. When I sit down with a cup of coffee, curl my feet under me, and open my Bible to read His letter to me, He is decidedly Ты—my Father, my Friend, my Confidant. But there I go again, capitalizing the names of the Creator-King of all that is. Perhaps I will stick with my simple twenty-first century English "You," which encompasses both aspects. After considering its Russian counterparts, however, I will say, "You are my Lord and my God," with a greater awareness of both my Father (Ты) and my King (Вы).

NOTES:
[1] Isaiah 6:1.

[2] Exodus 24:15–18.

[3] Pascal, Blaise. Pensees. The Penguin Group, England, 1966.

[4] Isaiah 55:8–9.

[5] Hebrews 1:3.

[6] "Breathe." Directed by Rob Bell, produced by NOOMA, performance by Rob Bell. Zondervan, 2006. DVD.

[7] Davies, John. *A Song for Every Morning.* Canterbury Press, Norwich, England, 2008.

[8] Brown, R., and A. Gilman. "The Pronouns of Power and Solidarity." *Style in Language.* Edited by T. A. Sebeok. MIT Press, 1960.

See Questions and Activities, page 216.

Your Turn

Ask a question, record a thought, sketch a picture, compose a song, make an argument, draw a cartoon, pen a poem, or write a prayer.

If nothing comes to mind, read on.

A whisper...

It is Sunday afternoon. I decide to treat myself to a novel. I make a cup of tea and curl up on the couch with every intention of disappearing into my book. I open the cover and begin to get acquainted with the characters, but just as the story starts to get interesting, a line from its plain, black text turns unexpectedly to italics and jumps into a larger font. I gasp.

If I'd been fussing with the text on my computer, this would have been normal behavior for the letters, but this is just an ordinary book—a common mystery story about a lonely doctor who gets wrapped up in a secret she never ex- pected; its text is supposed to remain constant. But there He is...God has stepped right into the middle of my story with a sentence that, though it was certainly penned by the books' author, bears the unmistakable mark of God's inspiration. Right there between the comma and the period, He has diverted my attention so He could lovingly whisper His Presence into my ear.

Trip Report: Pikes Peak

I am now in South Carolina, and tomorrow I will walk into my first graduate class at Clemson University. I have been telling people that I am alternately excited and terrified. This is a new journey—a chance to step into a new season of life and an opportunity to serve God in a completely new way, in a new place, among a vastly different group of people than I've ever served before. It is a grand adventure. It is also frighteningly unfamiliar. I will be an old woman among twenty-five-year-olds; I will struggle with tech that they use intuitively; I will hold faith and values they consider old-fashioned and ridiculous. Will they accept me or dislike me? Will we be able to communicate, miss each other like ships in the night, or worse yet, offend one another?

The process of getting here has brought many frustrations. The last month seemed like swimming through molasses as I tried to get everything ready to leave, packing up our home of twenty-one years and facing unexpected medical issues which have, unfortunately, followed me to South Carolina. The final difficulty came when I spent the night before I had planned to leave sitting up with Captain, my seventeen-year-old Newfoundland, as he was dying. I spent the next day in tears and left twenty-four hours later than planned. I cried all the way to New Mexico.

Even so, it has seemed that every sermon, book, song, Bible lesson, and even every walk along the familiar roads of Beulah have held reminders and symbols that have opened my mind to new ways of looking at the path ahead. I have been in training all summer. I'd like to tell you about one particular "training session."

Two weeks before I left, David and I took a three-day climb up the Barr Trail to Pikes Peak as a celebration of our thirtieth wedding anniversary and a chance to climb one last mountain before I left Colorado. We arrived at the bottom of the Barr Trail at 6500 feet elevation just in time for a deluge of rain and hail. We huddled with other hikers beneath the eves of the last bathroom at the trailhead until the hail subsided. Dressed in rain gear, we started up the path, walking most of the way in what was now a running gully of mud and rocks.

We gained 2000 feet in the first 2 ½ miles of steep switchbacks, finally meeting the top of the Manitou Incline. It was a hard, wet climb, and I started to wonder why I had chosen *this* as our anniversary celebration; afterall, David had offered me a Marriot in Denver instead.

Still, we kept climbing, and it kept raining.

By mile three, the path had leveled out, though it was still making definite uphill progress. By mile marker 4 ½ I was tired—and tired of walking in wet shoes with my twenty-two-pound pack on my back. By mile marker six, I was wet and cold and just wanted to be at our campsite.

Finally—Barr Camp appeared ahead.

We arrived just in time to drop our packs and go into the cabin for dinner: spaghetti and dark garlic bread that reminded me of the soda bread we had enjoyed in Ireland. I am not usually a fan of spaghetti, but this tasted great. We checked into our lean-to (sort of a raised wooden tent, open to one side, but with the luxury of a real mattresses instead of sleeping on the ground). We rolled out our sleeping bags and hung our gear up to dry. Then we went back to the main cabin (which had solar power, and thus lights) and cuddled up on the couch to read together before going to bed.

The weather report for the next day did not look promising: rain predicted to begin by 10:00 a.m. with thunderstorms by noon—not long enough to make the summit six miles and 4000 vertical feet away—especially not for me, as I am a slow climber. It was the kind of weather report that would normally have caused David to postpone a summit attempt to a different day for safety reasons—a climber's greatest fear is a thunderstorm.

As we lay in our sleeping bags trying to get warm enough to fall asleep, we discussed our alternatives. We could set out in the morning and see how far we got before the rain turned us around; we could climb in the rain as long as it didn't thunder (which definitely didn't sound like fun—I do not like wet feet!); or we could not try at all—just head back down the six miles to Manitou and go find that Marriot—with a hot tub! We didn't make a decision but chose to wait and see what morning looked like.

We woke to thick, whole-grain pancakes filled with apples and nuts and drenched in maple syrup. Barr Camp is definitely the luxury way to climb; most summit attempts begin with a little lukewarm water poured from a thermos over instant oatmeal. The sky was cloudy, but not yet dripping. We decided to see how far we could get before the rain set in, so we set off "down" the trail—actually, it was decidedly up since we had 4000 feet to gain over the next six miles. Somewhere in the second mile, after we had begun the first set of steep switchbacks, I had a little conversation with myself.

"It's really not that big a deal if I don't make the summit. This is supposed to be a fun anniversary celebration with David, and walking twelve miles up and down in the rain does not sound like fun. I can let this go. We'll just go as far as the A-frame (a landmark hut at tree line), look at the view, and go back to cuddle up and relax at Barr Camp for the rest of the day. It's not important that I make the summit."

All of a sudden, God broke into the string of justifications in my mind.

"Is it important that you graduate?"

I was taken by surprise. I hadn't even been thinking about grad school or the fact that I was on the brink of leaving for Clemson. I was just climbing the mountain and trying to keep breathing as the oxygen got thinner.

"Well...Yes," I sort of stammered aloud.

God spoke in no more specific words, but the sense of His Presence and the symbolic nature of this hike became more and more clear as I trudged upward. There were a dozen places where I would have turned back, except that I felt God had told me to make that summit and had promised to give me the strength to do so. The whole hike became a symbolic microcosm of grad school: It will be hard—a challenge at the edge of my capabilities. It will require persistence, will, and God's strength to finish it. I cannot do it without Him, but neither will I have to. In this climb up Pikes Peak, God was promising to hike through the next two years with me.

And despite the threatening skies, He held back the rain. We made the A-frame at about 10:00 to a sky full of gray, boiling clouds, but no deluge...and no thunder, which would have forced us to turn around. We climbed on above tree line. We would be exposed the rest of the way—a hard, slow, steep three miles over rocky, open terrain. I thought we should have reached each mile marker long before we actually passed it.

At one switchback, as we turned to look out over the panorama of layered mountains with Colorado Springs in the distance and swirling clouds above, I broke into tears. It is not unusual for me to cry with fatigue on the way to a summit, but this was not fatigue. I suddenly realized that I had to climb this high so I could look out over Colorado and say, "Goodbye." It brings the tears all over again as I sit here writing about it. David put his arms around me and I stood looking out over home through my tears.

We turned back to the trail: a mile and a half and 1400 feet to go. Like all fourteeners, it grew steeper, rockier, harder to breathe. At one mile to the top, the summit looked no nearer than it had at two miles. Could I make it? God had said to do it—so I kept trudging. The clouds continued to threaten, but it still didn't rain. At 500 feet below the summit, I began to feel nauseous and my head began to hurt. It worsened as I climbed—altitude sickness.

Finally, the last few switchbacks. We summited about 12:30. I'd made the top—my seventeenth summit. Most of all, I'd done what God had asked me to do—I'd graduated, at least symbolically.

But I felt terrible.

The Pikes Peak summit is like no other. Most are lonely mountaintops covered with rocks and peopled only by the few hikers who have gotten there ahead of us (and an occasional pika), but Pikes Peak can be reached by car, by shuttle, or by cog rail. It is a popular destination for Colorado Springs tourists. It is a circus on top with a gift shop, a restaurant, and its own signature donut bakery. I wanted none of it. I used the bathroom and put my head down on a table in the snack bar. I almost went to sleep while David bought a couple of bottles of fruit juice (his magic elixir for getting back down the mountain).

David woke me, poured half a bottle of grape juice down my throat, and steered me outside to take the requisite summit pictures. I really didn't want to start back down. If tickets on the cog hadn't been sold out since May, I would have happily accepted a ride. As it was, what goes up must come down, and David and I both knew I'd feel better five hundred feet down the hill, so we started our descent.

Still, no rain.

Going down did help the altitude sickness, but I'm even slower downhill than up, carefully placing my feet and protecting my knees (which always complain about the descending portion of a climb). At about a mile and a half, we heard the first thunder. We were on the open rock field— the "long switchback"—with nowhere to go but onward.

Thunder on a peak, with thousands of tons of rocks above us ready to avalanche if hit by lightning, is usually scary. This time, while I did have a sense of urgency that kept me trudging along toward the relative safety of tree line, I wasn't scared. I still felt a strong sense of God's protection. He told me to go on to the summit despite the threatening clouds; He held off the rain for more than

69

four hours beyond what is usually an amazingly accurate prediction; and I was still walking inside the umbrella of His promise. But I was tired…and slow…and the thunder kept rumbling. We could see a thunderstorm building off to our right.

It began to rain about mile marker two, and we paused to put on our rain gear. Then it stopped—we didn't get wet at all. Finally, we reached tree line, rested through a late lunch at the A-frame, then hiked on….and on….and on…and on. The next three miles felt like forever. By the time we came across the last meadow and David pointed out the wildflowers, I told him that they were pretty, but I didn't care. I was just looking for Barr Camp to appear around each bend.

Finally, about 5:45, it did; we were still dry. When we had made our reservations, Barr Camp had been full for Saturday, so David had brought his tent for us to sleep in the second night. When we arrived, however, God provided an added blessing.

"Hey, we saved the anniversary suite for you," Zach, the caretaker, called out as we climbed the steps to the cabin porch; he'd had a cancellation. The "anniversary suite" was a dormitory with about twenty other hikers, but I was truly grateful—a mattress to sleep on and no wet tent. It did, indeed, rain that night, but we were safe and dry inside the cabin.

The next morning after a leisurely breakfast of more of those wonderful pancakes, we said goodbye to the caretakers and headed down the mountain toward Manitou. I was very tired from the previous day, but in good spirits. The weather prediction, however, was even worse than the day before. Rain on the way down was inevitable.

The first three miles were very pleasant, but the fact that we were on the last few of the twenty-four-mile roundtrip began to catch up with me. Carrying the pack got harder, and

I began to stumble. At four miles, I fell—twice—and became even slower as I stepped more carefully. I prayed again for no injuries. I kept looking for the 4 ½-mile marker and kept trudging. Had I missed it? No, my estimation of mileage is terrible when I'm tired.

Still, no marker. We were dropping altitude rapidly. Finally, we passed the 5½-mile marker. Somehow, we had missed noticing both the 4½- and the five-mile posts. Of course, we had actually walked the whole distance, but it felt as if God had taken a mile out of the trek for me.

Suddenly we were down! We walked the easy, flat half-mile to the shuttle stop and were soon at the car. It hadn't rained the whole way. We got into my Buick and headed for home.

Then the sky opened up.

Now, after a three-day drive, I find myself far away from Pikes Peak and Colorado and David. Here in South Carolina, I am preparing to climb another summit, four semesters in elevation. I suspect I will experience rocky trails, steep climbs, and fatigue—maybe altitude sickness of another kind. I will, however, not be hit by any storm violent enough to turn me back; I walk under God's umbrella. I suspect that I will also discover panoramas of understanding I have never seen before, fresh ideas blowing in the wind, and delicate southern flowers springing from under rocks along the path. I have much to learn. God and (after a brief time apart) David will walk the trail by my side all the way to this new summit.

See Questions and Activities, page 218.

Your Turn

Ask a question, record a thought, sketch a picture, compose a song, make an argument, draw a cartoon, pen a poem, or write a prayer.

If nothing comes to mind, read on.

Raw Deal

Author's note:

Most of my writing undergoes revision and editing and re-revision before I publish it in any public venue, and I teach my composition students that revising is key to good writing. This piece is an exception.

As the title suggests, it is raw. Occasionally, the emotions vying to pour themselves onto the page simply won't tolerate the conventions of grammar and style. Here, I've made only a few changes for clarity from what I tapped out on the keypad of my phone as I sat on the grass outside my doctor's office.

RAW

9/27/17

It's a hard day. School work is behind. I've been frustrated. And now a cancer diagnosis. It's a hard day. Life is full of hard days. And sweet days when everything is perfect. Hard times and sweet times. One year ago was one of those sweet times. Ireland, Scotland, London, Prague, Slovakia, Kazakhstan. Two and half weeks exploring the world with my husband. Enjoying life, seeing new things. Adventuring, wondering, exploring, finding. A week on my own in Eastern Europe finding out what I could do—confidence building. Learning, figuring out, puzzling, enjoying. Two weeks of teaching in Kazakhstan. What a joy. What a gift. My first time in a Russian-speaking country. Talking to students. Struggling with language. It was an extraordinary six weeks following an extraordinary summer. Wow. Then I came home in mid-October and the fires started—literally. Two evacuations. David dealt with the first one alone. And then a change to figurative fires, and it hasn't slowed down since: The decision to go for a master's degree—ten applications. Acceptance by Clemson. Acceptance of Clemson. A summer preparing. A death. A trip. And then the poker game started in July: Medical issues. More tests. An emergency room visit. Lots of dumb stuff I had to do. Most of them resolved—most of the tests were negative. Just dumb stuff I had to do. But one won't go away. A little more and a little more and a little more. It followed me to Clemson. I wanted to leave it behind. More tests. Trying to get my head above water in school. Trying to keep up with the 22-year-olds. Enjoying it, but sometimes too dumb to be here. Too dumb to live in the twenty-first century. The old-fashioned skills I brought to school don't count. I can't interface them with anyone else. Frustration. And then today, the poker game was moved to the back room where the high stakes are played. A cancer diagnosis. It's a bad day. But there will be other days. Another perfect day. It's God's day. Whether it's a perfect day in Ireland or the day of a cancer diagnosis. It's God's day. And I will pray to Him and trust Him, that there will be another day. Another perfect day.

Another note:
> *That raw swirl of thoughts distilled itself into a poem which became the image on which I took my stand and held my ground in the months that followed my diagnosis.*

DEAL!

This isn't penny ante anymore.
It's a high-stakes, back-room poker game,
and I'm all in.
But I do not bet alone.
Behind me stands
the One who holds all the cards,
while I sit across the table
from an adversary
who only knows how to bluff.

So, go ahead…*deal!*

See Questions and Activities, page 219.

Your Turn

Ask a question, record a thought, sketch a picture, compose a song, make an argument, draw a cartoon, pen a poem, or write a prayer.

If nothing comes to mind, read on.

Cancer, Comfort, and Calling

As a new graduate student (and an old one—well-aged, I mean), I am finding opposite extremes in the varied views of God that surround me.

On one hand, among the wide variety of material that I am reading for my Medieval Literature class, (including Aristotle, a character from Melville who dies from nothing-ness, assorted philosophers, and the love poems—sometimes lust poems—of medieval troubadours) appear several medieval religious thinkers and monastics. Their writings analyze God, praise Him, attempt to prove Him, and search for their place in Him. Some describe the world as, at best, a distraction and, at worst, an evil to be disdained and abstained from. One in particular, Marguerite Porete, be-lieves that to draw nearer to God she must separate herself entirely from the joys, cares, and sorrows of the world, completely annihilating her own will until she desires nothing, despises nothing, needs thing—until she has no passions at all and is entirely swallowed up in the will of God. She wishes to be neither influenced nor affected by the world, so that her entire focus may be on God[1].

On the other hand, I am surrounded by academics and contemporary young people who see God as, at best, passe and inconsequential, an object of literary or cultural study; or, at worst, a tool in the hands of an evil bourgeoisie—Marx's opiate to be fought against. They are fully entrenched in the world with all its problems, inconsistencies, and injustices, and feel a humanist obligation to fix it. Many simply don't see God at all, immersing themselves in the distractions and entertainments of social media and college life. (It has been said that the devil need not make us evil if he can, instead, make us busy with things that have no eternal consequence—a great variety of which are at our fingertips on the internet).

And yet, God is here—right in the middle of all these opinions. And so am I. He does call me to spend time on the porch with Him in the company of the woodchuck, the scarlet cardinal, and the intricately-painted blue jays who frequent my backyard. Here, I can listen, learn, and grow closer to Him, but He also bids me to leave the porch and walk, not away from Him, but with Him into a world in need of His love.

He asks me not to disdain, but to truly and deeply love *all* of the people around me with His Love (occasionally I succeed). Some of those people share my faith: I have so appreciated the notes and prayers of my far-away friends from home; I have found a very caring and supportive church; and surprisingly, as a result of my cancer, I am discovering an amazing number of fellow Christians at school. The kitten card one young colleague sent with a very sincere prayer "for God's healing and peace" made me smile and lifted my spirits.

I believe that God does, at times, call people to full-time, full-immersion prayer—the separated monastic life that Porete coveted being one example—but that is not my call. I am called to love and, as the cancer is teaching me, to allow myself to be loved by a world full of people who are *all* loved by Him.

At first, I planned to keep my breast cancer diagnosis close to the chest (pun definitely intended) and not to tell too many people. However, again and again, that has not seemed to be the appropriate approach. As I have let it be known, I have found Christians in places I didn't expect and a level of care and sympathy among non-Christians that breaks down the dividing walls and allows Love to speak in both directions.

I was diagnosed just before October, which is breast cancer awareness month. Not long afterward, a group of activist undergrads were manning a table on the library bridge handing out pink ribbons. As I walked by, a young man stepped into the flow of foot traffic to offer me a ribbon. Being still a bit raw, I told him, "No, thank you," and added that I'd just been diagnosed and wasn't ready to deal with the ribbon thing yet. He immediately drew me aside and called in a young lady from the group by the table. He said, "I don't know what religion you are, but can we pray for you?" And they did, right there in the middle of the crush of students heading to their next class. The following day, the same young man chased me into the library to tell me that the entire Fellowship of Christian Athletes had prayed for me the night before.

If God intended me to annihilate my will as Porete

suggests, and to spend all of my time and energy on my knees before Him, He could end my life and take me to where worship would be my only job. So far, at least, He hasn't done that. If I were intended to spend all my time and energy striving to fix the injustices of the world and bringing about revolutionary changes, He would not constantly demonstrate my inability to affect any kind of change without His help. Rather, He asks me to let Him bring my will into harmony with His and to offer my hands in collaboration with His plans to bring about the changes He sees as necessary.

That doesn't mean I have no desires of my own. I would be lying if I said I don't care about going through cancer treatment. I still don't want to do this, but I will take His hand and walk through it, letting Him transform the experience through the crucible of Romans 8:28 into whatever He intends it to be, and I will do my best to love the people around me with an intense, consuming passion fueled by His love for them...and for me.

NOTES:

[1] Porete, Marguerite, *The Mirror of Simple Souls*. Translated by Ellen L. Babinsky. Paulist Press, 1993. Originally written in the late fourteenth century; First published in 1927.

See Questions and Activities, page 221.

Your Turn

Ask a question, record a thought, sketch a picture, compose a song, make an argument, draw a cartoon, pen a poem, or write a prayer.

If nothing comes to mind, just turn the page.

A fragrance . . .

I've had enough for one day, so I'm leaving the meeting early. After a few blocks of walking, I have almost arrived at my car when I am stopped short. A wave of scent washes over me, thick and sweet. The air is heavy with the fragrance; something nearby must be in full flower. I look all around, but I can see nothing—only evergreens and leafy bushes with no color or hint of blossoms. Where is that aroma coming from? And why didn't I notice it an hour ago when I got out of my car in this same spot? Somewhere an out-of-sight, tree-sized bouquet is pouring its perfume onto the passing breeze.

I smile. This has happened before. It is just God's way of sending me flowers and reminding me that He is always standing nearby.

To Be or Not To Be

the Blind Man

As he passed by, he saw a man blind from birth. And his disciples asked him, "Rabbi, who sinned, this man or his parents, that he was born blind?" Jesus answered, "It was not that this man sinned, or his parents, but that the works of God might be displayed in him. We must work the works of him who sent me while it is day; night is coming, when no one can work. As long as I am in the world, I am the light of the world." Having said these things, he spit on the ground and made mud with the saliva. Then he anointed the man's eyes with the mud and said to him, "Go, wash in the pool of Siloam" (which means Sent). So he went and washed and came back seeing.

—John 9:1–7

I must admit that my first reaction to the story of Jesus healing the blind man in John 9 misses the whole point of Jesus' miracle. The disciples point out a blind beggar in the street and ask whether his malady is the result of his own sins or those of his parents—not a very compassionate question. It seems that, to them, this guy is not a hurting human being but merely a case study on which to hang a theological debate. Jesus quells the discussion by telling them that his blindness is not the result of anyone's sin, but rather is so that, "the works of God might be displayed in him."[1]

Wait a minute!!

I stop reading right there and find myself tripping over two competing reactions at the same time:

1) You mean God made this guy blind and subjected him to years of begging so that He could show off His power? That doesn't sound very compassionate or loving; and

2) Wow! How cool is that—to have "the works of God displayed"[1] in his life?!

On one hand, I feel sorry for the poor guy; on the other, I think I want God to demonstrate His power, grace, love and glory in my life too. Ah, but am I willing to embrace suffering to provide Him that opportunity?

Could it be that these aren't conflicting thoughts at all? For me to have compassion on the blind man puts me in the same camp with Jesus Himself. He didn't just discuss the theological underpinnings of the man's condition but stopped to administer a cure. As for God imposing the blindness on him in the first place, I don't think God inflicts disease, disaster, or distress on us, but He certainly does permit them. Why?

One of my graduate professors argued with me, asking how I could characterize God as loving when He punishes us cruelly for disobedience and allows innocents to suffer. It is a question people have been asking ever since Cain slew Able. He found my defense unconvincing and left the conversation concluding that I am naïve and must never have faced real fear, pain, or grief. Later, however, he sent me an email telling me that he had been brought up short in the produce section when he was buying blueberries after our discussion. He suddenly remembered that I had been fighting a cancer diagnosis throughout grad school. How, he wondered, could I feel loved by this God who has the power to heal, but allows me and those I care about to suffer?

I have to agree with him that misery certainly exists, and sometimes it seems very unfair. Few, if any, of us get through life without facing it on some level, but I don't see it as a punishment from God for which I should blame Him.

Bad things happen. They are a by-product of living on this side of The Garden.

Sometimes, as the disciples first assumed in the story about the blind man, these bad things come as the results of our own misdeeds. Other times, we are subject to the consequences of other people's selfishness: the sins of the people around us; the sins of those who are in power over us; the sins of those who've gone before us, either immediately or historically all the way back to Eden, where Adam and Eve's desire to be God for themselves plunged us all into a world of thorns and curses. Of course, it isn't only their fault; every generation since has affirmed their insult against God's sovereignty. Still, each misfortune we encounter provides an opportunity for God to bathe us in grace and reaffirm His promise to be Emmanuel, God with us.

Cancer was not something I would have chosen, but neither has God abandoned me to its affliction. Rather than seeing it as a punishment, I feel extraordinarily blessed. Have all the medical procedures been a time-consuming distraction? Yes. Are the side effects of the medication annoying? Yes. Would this whole graduate experience have been easier without the medical issues? Of course. Yet, throughout this whole journey, I have been aware of God walking by my side and even fashioning surprising blessings out of the medical mud from this unwanted road which we have trod.

Early on, David and I both had to think through and accept the fact that this could kill me. Though I am grateful that doesn't seem to be the path we're on, I remain at peace with the possibility. I view all the opportunities I've had in my life as tremendous privileges granted by the God who loves me.

An embroidered plaque that my eldest daughter made for me hangs on the wall in my office at home. It reads,

"Faith makes things possible, not easy."

God does not promise me a life free of difficulty or suffering. Rather, He promises to walk with me through whatever comes.

That is not just a platitude; it is my experience.

I guess maybe all of us are the blind man, bearing the various maladies of this world while God pours His grace over us until His glory glimmers from every crease and crinkle and crevice of our countenances.

How cool is that!

NOTES:
[1] John 9:4.

See Questions and Activities, page 222.

Your Turn

Ask a question, record a thought, sketch a picture, compose a song, make an argument, draw a cartoon, pen a poem, or write a prayer.

If nothing comes to mind, just turn the page.

The Author

Lord, You write my story
a few lines at a time;
You keep me on the edge of my seat,
turning page after page, day after day.
I am privileged to be a character,
walking through Your epic.
Some chapters set the stage;
some build tension;
some deal with crisis
or introduce fascinating new characters
to help me unravel the intrigue.
Others are comfortable denouements,
wrapping up loose ends
and providing a quiet breather,
before I am plunged
into the next twist of plot.
I do not know how the story will end,
but You do.
I will just keep on reading.

See Questions and Activities, page 223.

Your Turn

Ask a question, record a thought, sketch a picture, compose a song, make an argument, draw a cartoon, pen a poem, or write a prayer.

If nothing comes to mind, just turn the page.

The Song of a Lonely King

A dam and Eve hung out in the garden, sharing company, conversation, chores, and sex without dissension or dispute, and the Spirit of God walked the garden trails with them in the cool of the evenings. God Himself saw and declared that it was all good.

All except one thing: In the middle of the garden stood a tree—the Tree of the Knowledge of Good and Evil. If everything around them was good, why was there—indeed how could there have been—any concept, least of all "knowledge," of evil at all. Did the first couple even understand the meaning of the word? Did they have any mental hooks to hang the idea of badness on? Why did God, who is Goodness Himself, allow this suggestion of evil to remain in His perfect place? Why did He permit satan* to infiltrate His paradise in the guise of the serpent to bring the suggestion that choosing anything but God's carefully crafted plan was possible?

These were not accidents or oversights—this is God we are talking about: The Omniscient and All-powerful. These were intentional choices by the Divine. In the midst of all this good, God allowed evil to cast its shadow. Why?

Fast forward several thousand years to Solomon whose father was the great King David, a very powerful but also very human king who had repented from his own flirtations with evil (adultery and murder, to be exact). When Solomon stepped up to his father's throne (after a rather dramatic argument with a usurping brother), he, too, was both powerful and human. Though he had a reputation for extraordinary wisdom, not all of his policies were wise; personally, I wouldn't have wanted to live under his tax code.

As king, he also enjoyed the trappings of royalty: a palace that truly *was* built for a king, servants and officials who carried out his every wish, the command of a large and well-equipped army, and wives—seven hundred of them, plus a few stray concubines. No young woman in his realm could refuse the king—at least it wouldn't have been a good idea. Everyone did his bidding, whether it involved what he wanted for dinner, what color the hangings of the new temple should be, or whom he would be sleeping with that evening.

Solomon was a man who had, or could have, anything he wished for, but his life was not without frustration or depression. It was, indeed, *this* king, reputed to be the wisest man who had ever lived, who at the end of his life wrote in Ecclesiastes, "When I considered all that my hands had done and the toil I had expended in doing it, and behold, all was vanity and a striving after wind, and there was nothing to be gained under the sun."[1]

It was also Solomon to whom the Bible's premier love story, the Song of Solomon (titled Song of Songs in some versions) is attributed. In this hot-blooded tale, the king (often assumed to be Solomon himself) is involved in a steamy courtship and marriage with a young woman we know only as his "Shulammite Bride."[2] The inclusion of Song of Songs in the biblical cannon has been a puzzle to many and an embarrassment to some.

For several thousand years, theologians have attempted to explain, justify, and come to peace with what, at least on first glance, appears to be a very sensual, even sexual narrative. Some commentators have accepted it as just that: a steamy account of an actual love affair between Solomon and a beloved wife (though they disagree on which wife she was). They suggest that the purpose behind Song of Songs is to picture and emphasize the sacred importance of marriage.

Others have stepped over the sensual nature of the literature (at times turning verbal back handsprings to pretend the book's more sexual comments don't mean what they appear to say) to focus on a more symbolic or allegorical approach. They suggest that the story is about the spiritual relationships between God and the Jewish people, Christ and the church, the Holy Spirit and Mary, or God and each individual beloved believer. Others insist that both approaches are true, and that this enigma of biblical literature is doing its work on a variety of levels simultaneously.[3]

I don't wish to question three thosand years of biblical scholarship, nor would I want to argue with the likes of John of the Cross, Gregory the Great, or Thomas Aquinas.

Still, I wonder…

Imagine Solomon, the Israelite king who has had the task of designing and building God's temple handed down to him by his iconic father. This was a man who was very conversant with symbols of the Divine and could certainly have written a spiritual parable. He was also a political king who ruled over the most peaceful era in Jewish history. He was in the business of making deals and establishing alliances. That, in fact, is where some of his many wives came from— using marriages to seal political deals was a pretty common practice. He *could* have fallen madly in love with one of them and recorded the account of their affair in his amorous poem.

But what if Song of Songs grew out of a completely different element of Solomon's experience.

What if Solomon wrote it not as an intentional parable nor as an account of his own relationship with a favorite wife, but as a fantasy—a personal romance novel written out of the longings of a lonely king? Perhaps the man in Song of Songs was, indeed, the writer himself, but what if the woman we've never been able to positively identify never existed at all?

I know that in many circles, my suggestion that part of the Bible isn't merely metaphorical, but is actually imaginary may be met with cries of heresy (though some have made similar claims about the book of Job). Still, I will ask you to please bear with me for a few minutes more before lighting the sticks beneath the heretic's stake.

By the end of his life, we are told that Solomon was the husband of seven hundred wives,[4] but Song of Songs was written early in his reign when his harem held only "sixty queens and eighty concubines..." and of course, "virgins without number."[5]

So, what was it like to be one of Solomon's wives? I do not think any surviving literature gives a direct answer, but perhaps the story of Esther, though it takes place some years after Solomon in the court of the Persian king, Ahasuerus, can shed some light on the way this harem thing worked in the ancient Near East. Beautiful girls from throughout the realm and beyond were brought into the harem and prepared for the king. After spending a night with their kingly husband, many of them returned to the chambers of the wives to live out the remainder of their lives. Even if he did request their company again, how often could they have been called, with 699+ other women about?

Could it be that over time, Solomon, the king who could have any woman he wanted, as long as she wasn't previously married to someone else (Solomon's parents had broken that rule and the results had been dire), grew frustrated and dissatisfied with this unending stream of beautiful virgins? Could it be that in practice, serial wives are not much different from serial hook-ups which eventually become empty, even boring? Could it be that, in the end, polygamy is not all it is cracked up to be?

What if this well-sexed king, who later in life wrote, "There is nothing new under the sun,"[6] became the loneliest man in the palace? Despite his many wives, Solomon lacked what Adam had—a partner. Could it be that Solomon longed for something deeper—a relationship that could satisfy not only his body but also his heart and his soul?

And so, on one solitary night, the king goes into his chamber, not with the latest hot brunette in harem pants, but rather with a bottle of ink and a blank scroll. There he begins to dream on paper (or rather, on vellum). He imagines a woman not dressed in palace finery, but with her skin burned by the sun after spending her days working in the vineyard—a commoner, unaccustomed to royal etiquette. He dips his pen, but hesitates for a moment, chewing on its end. Who is she?

She is someone he can go secretly to visit, joyfully bounding over the hills like a young stag on his way to her house, rather than having her simply brought to his chamber. He can slip out to see her alone, without his entourage of bodyguards and officials. The sudden thought of her in the midst of a state meeting might make him catch his breath and hide his smile behind a piece of official parchment. Recalling the silhouette of her body could render him breathless for a moment and make his heart race even when he is sitting still.

But what might she think of this king who was coming to call? Could she love him—really love *him*? Solomon dips the pen again and starts to write in careful Hebrew letters from right to left across the top of the scroll. He begins his fantasy with her voice as he imagines her imagining him: "Let him kiss me with the kisses of his mouth!"[7]

But her passion is not a love he can demand; he must deserve her devotion. Here is a woman whose hand he can take timidly, his own fingers tingling at the anticipation of her touch. She is not commanded by his every wish; she can run away if she chooses. This is a woman he must court, cater to, invite. He can take her flowers, not knowing if she will accept them...or him.

This is a woman who can say no.

For her amusement, he can point out the beauty of the hills, the gazelles, the birds, and the lilies just to watch the scarlet ribbon of her lips break into a smile. He can ask her to run with him to their own secret spot in the woods and to lay beside him under a canopy of pines. He prays that she will indeed let him kiss her with his mouth and hold her in his arms, reveling in her presence, her warmth, the curve of her breast, the fragrance of her hair against his cheek.

Solomon continues to scratch on the scroll. There will be no sleep for him tonight. The king is entranced. He never tires of picturing her dove-like eyes, her hair tumbling over her shoulders like a flock of goats running down a hillside, her dainty breasts that remind him of twin gazelles. Her eyes overwhelm him, and the spicy scent of her frankincense overcomes the thoughts of everything else in his realm. The milk and honey of God's promises are hiding under her tongue. This mystical lady is a "garden locked,"[8] the one for whom he must wait and wish and yearn. He cannot order this woman but waits for her invitation.

Of course, in his fantasy, she does return his adoration. She calls him radiant and runs her fingers through his raven-black hair and whispers her appreciation of his polished chest "bedecked with sapphires."[9] Here, finally, is the woman who doesn't love the king, but loves *him*.

He longs to get to know her little by little over a period of years, exploring the idiosyncrasies that make her unique. He wants to find out what she most enjoys, what she thinks about, what she dreams of. He wishes for adventures that only they know about—perhaps a spontaneous picnic where the wild apples and apricots and raisins are sufficient to become a banquet because of the love in which they are shared. He makes up the stories she might tell him about the funny things that happen in her day or the dreams she has at night. He imagines sharing his own frustrations or the mysterious occurrences he's seen or the things that have saddened him.

Solomon's other wives are his, but he is not theirs. This is a woman of whom he could truly say "I am my beloved's."[10]

Solomon's handwriting grows a bit shaky as he pours

his desire onto the scroll, describing his courtship, her adoring response, their marriage, and their lives together. Here on the soft vellum, Solomon finds the one woman who will never live in his harem—the woman he can never have, but who commands his fascination with an intensity no harem wife has ever matched. She is Solomon's ideal Dulcinea because she loves him by her own choice.

This reading of Song of Songs remains true to the literal images that adorn the pages of Solomon's beautiful love poem, and it does nothing to depreciate the value or power of Song of Songs as a spiritual narrative, nor does it contradict our understanding that Scripture is divinely inspired. In fact, the idea of Solomon sighing as he writes, in concert with God, a story that simultaneously describes the human longings of one and the Divine desires of the Other seems more a product of heavenly inspiration than the simple recounting of a love affair.

Just as we recognize Ecclesiastes as the musing of an elderly king looking back over his life, why couldn't Song of Songs be the yearning of a younger sovereign, wishing for a woman who could forget he was the king? Such an interpretation underscores both the importance of a meaningful and loving marriage between life-long lovers and the figurative commentary on God's relationship with his church and His people. Indeed, the romantic longings of the king of Judah might shed much light on the heart of the King of all creation. What if this fantasy of a lonely king is also a picture of a creating God who, like Solomon, wishes for a real relationship rather than a court filled with yes-men and women?

Perhaps here, we must return to Eden.

Could it be that God, too, wanted a relationship with

someone who could say no? That He wanted to court us, to woo us, to demonstrate His love for us in the breathless hope that we would *choose* to love Him back? Perhaps God didn't want us to be concubines who were brought to Him in submission whether we wanted to follow or not. Did he plant that Tree of the Knowledge of Good and Evil in his perfect garden so that we would have an alternative? He longed for a bride who could refuse Him, and whose love, if she chose to come into His embrace, would be returned to Him with the same intense eagerness as His own love for her. This is a story about a Deity who loves us completely, deeply, passionately (after all, Christ's crucifixion is called His Passion). He wishes to be loved in return with that same passion and intensity.

So, what is it to be God's lover? To be kissed by Him and anointed in His perfume? To sit in His chamber with His full attention? Not only to speak the name of God, but to hear it as it pours like oil from my own lips? To have Him take my hand and lead me across the hills? A human suitor might point out the flowers and figs and foxes, inviting his beloved to enjoy the natural beauty which his lover's eye has brought into sharper focus, but what if that Lover is God the Creator? Would the beauty surrounding me suddenly become not just wonders to be discovered and shared, but a masterpiece crafted just for me—not just a view, but a gift. Perhaps in that moment, He would not be saying, "Isn't this beautiful; come enjoy it with Me," but rather, "Look what I've made for you."

A human lover might bring a bouquet of roses; *this* Lover brings all the roses the world can produce, along with every snow capped mountain, every pouring waterfall, and every endless grassland populated by birds that chirp and sing and caw and call. All because He loves us. Loves me. How can I receive such an extravagant present? I could turn it down—but why would I? I doubt that I could ever be worth such a love, but here He is loving me. All I can do is melt into His arms and receive His gifts.

Solomon, as the romantic novelist, wishes to be enthralled, encompassed, intoxicated, captured, not only by his bride's beauty (though he is clearly taken with her ravishing appearance) but by the experience of being with her—by a desire that will last beyond the bedroom. It is not just the look of her that delights him, but the way she looks at him. This imaginary woman isn't just one of the harem; she is uniquely one.

If I read Song of Songs with God in the Lover's role, I must then realize that the God who is capable of commanding anything to happen instantly at His word, waits expectantly for my decision. In that waiting does God long for me? Is He delighted when I stop what I am doing and glance His way? Can it be that I hold the spices and fragrant flowers that can enthrall the One who created them? Does He wait for me to choose Him, not because He couldn't command me, but because He has bound Himself not to?

How could I not love such a lover?

In Song of Songs, the lovers lay together on a deep, green, earthy carpet. He leans his head against her breast and they revel in the quiet. It is the sweet enjoyment of the Lover and the beloved sitting in silence and murmurs, oblivious to the rest of the world, comparing each other to the natural wonders that enhance their time together.

I have certainly enjoyed such moments with my husband, surrounded by a thrilling calm that notices no other obligations. I have also enjoyed such moments in prayer with God. I sit like Solomon's lady, cuddled into God's chest, completely tranquil, and yet strangely exhilarated by the sense of His all-encompassing and all-consuming love for me. I pray, knowing that He already knows everything about me, but aware that He wants to hear my voice speak of my concerns, my questions, my joys. I am comfortable that I have nothing I need to hide from Him. When it is time to get up from my chair to go on with the responsibilities of life, I am loathe to leave.

Lying in David's arms or sitting in prayer with God—I find the two experiences remarkably similar.

Yet, like the bride in Solomon's poem, I recognize myself as just one lily in a field of lilies, nonunique and unimportant until the God of the universe picks me out and makes me special. Yet the characters in Song of Songs include not only the bride and the bridegroom, but also their friends. They too are encouraged to search for and love the Beloved.

God loves me as if I am the only one, and yet at the same time I am part of the great chorus that loves Him too. We praise Him together, but He delights in each of us as His one and only. God can do what Solomon with his many wives could not: He can love every one of us with an incomparable intimacy and passion. His is a love so vast and complete that it can be showered over me in full abundance without slighting any of the other flowers around me.

Though I am His and He is mine, that does not in any way diminish the fact that Miriam and Maureen and Theresa and Chad and Martha and Emory, Lyssa, Quin, Kayla, Mark, Josiah, Alexis, Demarcus, Alex, Janice, Jenna, Chelsey, Torren, Aspen, Robert, Emilie, and Tavia...are also dearly loved by Him in the same deep, passionate way; nor does His love for them diminish my desire for Him.

Could this be why Scripture points out that Solomon had seven hundred wives? Somehow Solomon provides an image of the God who loves billions of us, and yet, does so with the same individual devotion and intensity with which the king loves the Shulammite. Can we love Him back as fully as she who is "drunk with love?"[11]

God is not lonely. He is complete in Trinity, and yet what He wants from us is that we love Him. That is, after all, the greatest commandment—that we love God with all that we are—yet it is a commandment we are free to break. God offers us His love; we can accept it or reject it or treat it as a passing fancy—an occasional one-night stand. We can engage Him when it suits us and then go on with the rest of our business, or we can long for Him, desire Him. We can, like Solomon's beloved bride, run through the streets and squares of our daily lives in search of the One our souls love. The thought of Him can excite us, draw us, energize us, empower us.

As I write these words I find myself breathless like the bride, excited and delighted, even exuberant at the thought of this glimpse of God, the Lover, and at the prospect of being seen and adored by Him.

Some may find my sexual interpretation inappropriate, but is it really so odd to imagine that if I am loved, really loved, by One described as "the consuming fire,"[12] that the sexual intensity Solomon attempts to portray could, in fact, be merely a pale suggestion of what His holy love is really like? To be the object and recipient—the beloved—of the One whose very person defines love itself, implies a love beyond what even Solomon could envision.

This is a picture of the God who asks me to love Him

voluntarily. Thus, like Solomon's lover, my vineyard is mine to give or not to give. Could he take it? Of course. To suggest otherwise would be to belie the definition of "all powerful"—but He doesn't. He prefers to wait and let me choose, because in that choice I find myself able to say with the bride:

"I am my Beloved's and my Beloved is mine."[13]

NOTES:

[1] Ecclesiastes 1:4.
[2] Song of Solomon 6:13.
[3] Tanner, Paul J. "The History of the Interpretation of the Song of Songs." 1997. Web. Feb 2, 2019.
[4] 1 Kings 11:3.
[5] Song of Solomon 6:8.
[6] Ecclesiastes 1:9.
[7] Song of Solomon 1:2.
[8] Song of Solomon 4:12.
[9] Song of Solomon 5:14.
[10] Song of Solomon 7:10.
[11] Song of Solomon 5:1.
[12] Deuteronomy 4:24.
[13] Song of Solomon 6:3.

*The lack of capitalization here is not a typo. In English, we capitalize names. It is a form of honor given to anyone or anything important enough to be named specifically. God receives special honor in our writing, as not only His name is capitalized, but also pronouns and sometimes adjectives or other nouns that refer directly to Him. I offer no such honor to the evil one, thus even his name remains lower case.

See Questions and Activities, page 224.

Your Turn

Ask a question, record a thought, sketch a picture, compose a song, make an argument, draw a cartoon, pen a poem, or write a prayer.

If nothing comes to mind, just turn the page.

A sigh . . .

*It is a very special occasion. I find myself in the
midst of a rare gathering of my grown children
who all live far from us as well as far away
from one another. As we get reacquainted and
update each other on the events of our individual
lives, I watch the old patterns from their
childhoods reassert themselves. Soon everyone
is trying to talk at once while sharing stories,
cracking jokes, and teasing each other with
embarrassing memories from long ago. The
laughter grows louder and louder.*

*Then I seem to hear another voice in the crowd;
God has joined us in our merriment—after all,
He is the founder of this family.*

In the Playroom

I stand in the middle of the floor, a tiny child in the playroom. Around me lay my toys: a matchbox car that really does go "vroom vroom" down the road; picture books that tell animated stories of real or imagined places—I'm not always sure I know the difference; pick-up-sticks that I never pick up. My Legos lay scattered about the floor—bricks with which I try to construct architecture and sculptures like my Father's. What I build remains stiff and square with lots of rough edges; His are smooth and supple. They glow with color and breathe with life.

Sometimes, I am a misbehaved little girl. Here I sit, trying to imitate my Father's harmony and design and color and poetry, while I treat the people in my life, who are wonderful creations of His, like toy dolls, expecting them to say the words I tell them to say and do what I ask. When they don't, I get angry and break them. Or I abandon them, leaving them alone and strewn about the floor among the other toys. My

Father is happier when I pick them up and care for them as playroom friends.

Over there, under the window is a pile of crayons and colored pencils. I use them to draw stick figures of lions with pointy ears and long whiskers or spotted cows with cartoon bubbles that say, "Moo." I try to copy my Father's menagerie of creatures, but my simple imitations can never begin to match what He can do with just a breath.

Oh yes, there's the toy piano that plinks out childish songs and poems, trying to add a tiny strain to my Father's universal symphony.

Occasionally, I gather up the bright-blue satin dress-up gown that lays crumpled in the corner. With it I cover my ordinary clothes and pretend, for a few minutes, to be a princess.

Yet when I raise my eyes from the playroom floor— when I look up into my Father's face in the heavens—He is not disappointed with my feeble efforts or my childish games. He is pleased when I try to imitate Him—to follow His acts of creation—though my powers to design are so much silliness compared with His.

He reaches down and invites me to take His hand so that He can guide me on a tour of the real universe He is constantly creating all around me. He shows me the rocks and trees and mountains, the desert flowers and ocean froth and snowy peaks. He points out His favorite masterpieces of all—the real people walking around His world, breathing, moving, and creating with Him. He shows me their works of art, too—still no match for His, but wonderful attempts, with which He is pleased.

We return to the playroom; I look across the carpet. These are the tools and materials He has put into my life so that I can create with Him. I guess I don't always take very good care of them. Together we clean up the playroom floor and put everything in its place so it doesn't get spoiled or broken, and so I can find each gifted item when I need it.

Then the King of heaven, who created all that is, kneels on the floor beside me. He picks up a purple crayon and puts it in my hand. As I sit on the floor—crisscross applesauce—and lean over a bright yellow piece of construction paper, He places His huge, warm hand over my little one, and we begin to draw a sunset. He helps me find the words to describe it in a hand-scrawled poem at the bottom of the page. With His help, I too begin to create—to co-create—with Him. And He smiles at my efforts.

I look down and realize that I am still wearing the blue satin dress-up gown. That's okay, because I really am a princess, a daughter of the King.

See Questions and Activities, page 225.

Your Turn

Ask a question, record a thought, sketch a picture, compose a song, make an argument, draw a cartoon, pen a poem, or write a prayer.

If nothing comes to mind, read on.

The Strong Nuclear Force

For several hundred years, deistic philosophers have suggested that God did, indeed, create the world and breathe life into human beings, but afterward He had more important things to attend to than babysitting us, so He moved on and let the world march slowly onward of its own volition. This theology of the King-who-has-abdicated-the-throne affords us a great deal of freedom, but little guidance or comfort. We are left with only our own wisdom to draw from, which, based on our historical behavior and current global condition, is not very reassuring.

My eldest daughter is a both a chemist and a nurse. In her scientific appraisal of the world, she finds no evidence of this disinterested God. Rather, she speaks of seeing God's fingerprints everywhere she looks. His Presence is clearly demonstrated even in the center of every single atom.

Imagine with me, for a moment, a common elementary school science experiment. In your mind's eye, take two bar magnets and lay them on a smooth table. Press the positively charged ends of the two magnets together (it will take a little effort). Keep holding on to one of the magnets but let go of the other. What happens? The free magnet shoots away from the stationary magnet with significant force.

It is the same with everything else in the universe—like charges repel each other—except in the center of an atom. There, a bunch of positively charged protons cuddle up together, leaving all of their negatively charged partners swirling around outside. They *should* fly apart—but they don't.

Scientists tell us that they are held together by the strong nuclear force. According to HyperPhysics from Georgia State University, "A force which can hold a nucleus together against the enormous forces of repulsion of the protons is strong indeed."[1] While a variety of theories try to explain the cause of the strong nuclear force, no one knows exactly what it is. Scientists can calculate its strength—and they have used it to develop nuclear bombs, nuclear power, and nuclear medicine—but they still can't fully explain it.

I suggest that Paul explains it in Colossians: "For in him all things were created: things in heaven and on earth, visible and invisible, whether thrones or powers or rulers or authorities; all things have been created through him and for him. He is before all things, and in him all things hold together."[2]

"In him all things hold together."

I think that is literally true. The force of God Himself keeps the atoms intact so that everything in our world remains as we expect it to be—so that my coffee cup continues to contain coffee; so that my chair continues to hold me up; so that the roof continues to keep out the rain. By His hand, despite the pull of the negative particles outside, God holds the nucleus of every atom together, creating the building blocks for everything we see and everything we are.

No, I don't think ours is an absent nor a disinterested God; we have His full and undivided attention all the time. Without it, our world would simply explode.

Nor are atoms the only things held together by God's strong nuclear force. The same is true of our families. We have created a whole bunch of like particles. In ways our kids would not want to admit, they are like us. Even when they pull against us, even when they try on other ideas, even when they pick up attitudes from their peers, they remain like us in very profound and fundamental ways. They have learned what we have taught them—it is part of who they are. Sometimes I have to admit this means I've managed to pass on some of the traits I don't like in myself—things I would have chosen not to give them—as well as the ones I wanted to teach, but good traits or bad, our kids are like us.

Just like the center of the atom, all of these like charges are trying to live together peacefully under one roof. It sometimes seems that the pull of all those repelling charges will tear our families apart, yet at our invitation, our Master Physicist is ready and waiting to intervene, applying His strong nuclear force to hold our nuclear families together as well.

An inanimate atom has no say in the matter, but God waits for our invitation before stepping into our family squabbles. As parents, may we pray diligently and constantly for our families, inviting the Great Scientist to use His power to hold us all together. May children pray for their parents as well.

Scientists tell us that the strong nuclear force is the strongest of the natural forces.[1] The same force from the hand of the same God who holds the atoms together can hold our families intact as well—don't underestimate it. Pray!

NOTES:
[1] Nave, C.R. "The Strong Force." HyperPhysics, 2017. http://hyper-physics.phy-astr.gsu.edu/hbase/Forces/funfor.html.
[2] Colossians 1:16–17 .

See Questions and Activities, page 226.

Your Turn

Ask a question, record a thought, sketch a picture, compose a song, make an argument, draw a cartoon, pen a poem, or write a prayer.

If nothing comes to mind, just turn the page.

An Audience with the King

In the year that King Uzziah died I saw the Lord sitting upon a throne, high and lifted up; and the train of his robe filled the temple. Above him stood the seraphim. Each had six wings: with two he covered his face, and with two he covered his feet, and with two he flew. And one called to another and said: "Holy, holy, holy is the LORD of hosts; the whole earth is full of his glory!"

And the foundations of the thresholds shook at the voice of him who called, and the house was filled with smoke. And I said: "Woe is me! For I am lost; for I am a man of unclean lips, and I dwell in the midst of a people of unclean lips; for my eyes have seen the King, the LORD of hosts!"

Then one of the seraphim flew to me, having in his hand a burning coal that he had taken with tongs from the altar. And he touched my mouth and said: "Behold, this has touched your lips; your guilt is taken away, and your sin atoned for." And I heard the voice of the Lord saying, "Whom shall I send, and who will go for us?" Then I said, "Here I am! Send me."

—Isaiah 6:1–8

O ver and over, the Bible describes God as our King. Isaiah's vision of this overwhelming monarch fills him with trembling. The Psalms speak of the King of Glory coming in;[1] of the Lord sitting enthroned as King forever;[2] and of singing praises to God who is King of all the earth.[3] The prophets repeatedly predict the coming of our King, and from his birth, until the sign is placed over the cross at his death, Jesus is proclaimed to be the King of the Jews.[4] Finally, in Revelation, He is declared not only to be king, but King of kings.[5]

For those of us living under the democratic system of twenty-first century America, where we elect our president and can un-elect him four years later if we choose, this idea of an all-powerful king reigning forever is a little hard to swallow. In our modern political understandings, such a description smacks of despotism and tyranny. So, what is God trying to tell us when He calls Himself our King? How should we act before so powerful a leader?

Whether we are talking about the Caesars of first century Rome, the feudal lords of medieval Europe, the emperors of ancient China, or the monarchs of England and France, the kings of old were absolute rulers. The fate of their people was fully in their hands. If they took this responsibility seriously and cared for their subjects as children, their realms prospered. If they didn't care, everyone suffered. One way or the other, the power of the king was unquestioned and unquestionable.

Loyalty was demanded and received. Though some of those kings were despots, the office of the king held respect. People were, in fact, willing to live and sometimes to die for the honor and glory of their king and country. Those who fought in his majesty's service were asked to swear their allegiance to him. This was not the flip and often thoughtless allegiance we speak when we say the pledge to our flag. Their pledges were total—a commitment of their person, their labor, their honor, their property, and even their lives—and it was a bond for life.

Those historical kings were also judges, with the power of pardon and punishment in their hands. Again, some took this responsibility seriously, trying to dispense justice as best they could. Others were capricious, and the fate of the accused before them depended more on how the king's breakfast had settled than on any hope of justice.

In some cases, when an accused person came before the king, literally to beg for his life, he prostrated himself or was forced into a prostrate position—flat on the floor at the feet of the king. But why this position? Certainly, lying flat on one's face doesn't lend itself to making a persuasive case in one's own defense, nor even to easily answering the king's questions.

Webster defines to prostrate as "to reduce to submission, helplessness or exhaustion."[6] Thus, to lie prostrate was to acknowledge the king's total power. The king could choose, on a whim, to drop a sword and separate the head from the body with no resistance whatsoever. In this position, the accused was, in fact, offering his life.

Monks and religious men also used this prostrate position as they approached God, placing themselves in symbolic submission before the altar. Now, we moderns seldom feel the necessity of lying on our faces on our bedroom floors as we approach God in prayer, but perhaps we could learn something from those who understood His Kingship and offered themselves before Him with total vulnerability and nothing held back.

You see, in truth, none of us comes before God with any

case to make in our defense. The Bible tells us that "we have all become like one who is unclean, and all our righteous deeds are like a polluted garment. We all fade like a leaf, and our iniquities, like the wind, take us away."[7] These sound to us like harsh words, and we tend to say, "Wait a minute...I have done a few good things in my time." But if we are honest, each of us also knows the thoughts of selfishness and greed, of anger and jealousy, of ambition for ourselves, of pride and thoughtlessness toward others that cross our minds and cloud our hearts. We remember the good things we have done with selfish motives and the bad deeds we've covered over so that no one will know.

When we lay our flawed natures next to even the tiniest image of the character of our Holy God, we find no comparison—I have nothing of value to bring Him. I can offer no case in my own defense. I have neither logic nor examples to argue before Him, and the evidence only underscores my guilt.

Thus, I am left like the criminals of old—prostrate before my King and begging His mercy with no resistance or recourse. Psalm 22:6 says, "I am a worm and no man," and truly, I am. I have no just way to come before God except as the worm—flat on my face on the cold stones at His feet.

However, our King, unlike the capricious kings of old, holds not only complete authority and unrestrained power, but also complete goodness, unequaled love, and unreserved mercy.

Though I have nothing more to offer Him than the naked worm on the floor, He has already looked forward, seen my plight, and solved it. He has, in fact, taken the punishment for my selfishness on Himself, so that my divine debt is paid. He, who is completely Holy, has chosen to be merciful. He takes my hand and gently helps me up from that prostrate position on the floor. He stands me before Him, then dresses me in a righteousness that is not my own but is rather the robe of Christ himself. My King looks at me and sees not the worm, but His own child. He draws me near.

Then, like the knights of old who pledged themselves in total allegiance to their kings, I have the opportunity to pledge my fealty to my King, promising in grateful response to His mercy, that all of the life He's given back to me, all of the abilities He has bestowed on me, all of my possessions, hopes, and dreams are at His disposal. With such a pledge, the child of God, who was so recently but worm, is transformed again—this time into the knight who gives herself in humble and loyal service to her King.

My King then prepares me for the battle into which He will send me, dressing me in His own armor; protecting me with the helmet of His salvation and the breastplate of His righteousness; holding me securely with the belt of His truth; and safeguarding my feet from the rocks and thorns of the trail with shoes of His peace. He arms me with the shield of faith and the sword of His spirit and His Word.[8] Then He marks me with His symbol and grants me a place under His standard. I kneel before Him to receive my marching orders for the day.

I know that the battle will not be easy. I may come back battered and bruised with my robe torn and my armor bloodied, yet I am willing to go into battle for the honor and glory of my King. I know that at the end of the day, He will take me in, heal my wounds, replace my equipment, and ready me to go out again tomorrow, for the battle is long, but I serve a King who is already victorious.

By myself, I am nothing but the worm before Him, but lifted in His loving arms, I become His heir: knighted, equipped, and ready for His mission.

God is, of course, more than a king. He is also the Lion and the Lamb and the Father and the Judge and the Servant and the Vine—all of these and many more. On other days, perhaps one of these images will be more helpful in drawing me near and helping me to understand this God whom I worship. It may be easier, at times, to talk to the gentle Shepherd, to cuddle into the arms of the loving Father, or to sit in the shade beneath the life-giving Vine, but today, I will approach Him as my King, offering myself as a loving child and a loyal knight and saying, "My Lord, I am at your service."

NOTES:

[1] Psalm 24:7–10.
[2] Psalm 29:10.
[3] Psalm 47:2, 6–7.
[4] Matthew 2:2; Mark 15:26; Luke 23:38; John 19:19.
[5] Revelations 17:14.
[6] "Prostrate," *Merriam-Webster*, 2020.
[7] Isaiah 64:6.
[8] Ephesians 6: 14–17.

See Questions and Activities, page 227.

Your Turn

*Ask a question, record a thought, sketch a picture, compose a song,
make an argument, draw a cartoon, pen a poem, or write a prayer.*

If nothing comes to mind, read on.

Breakfast

I worship at the feet of the One who first imagined a sky full of glittering stars, who told the sun to start shining, and who built the mountains I like to climb. He cares for each sparrow and holds every atom in its place. He creates by simply speaking, and His thoughts are so far beyond my ken that I can't even find the right questions to ask Him, yet He comprehends the cry of a tiny baby. I am awed and humbled.

Yet, as I sit in adoration of this great Creator King, I also lay my head in the lap of my gentle Father, for I am, indeed, a daughter of this King. Even as He directs the weather, keeps all the planets spinning in proper time, and answers the prayers of billions, He has time to delight in my stories, to laugh at my silly antics, and to correct me when I get out of line. He invites me to sit at His table, conversing freely as we share a simple breakfast.

I was royal by birth—conceived by His own hand, carefully knit together, fearfully and wonderfully designed[1]—but I walked away and declared my independence, rejecting my position as His princess. When I was hopelessly lost and frightened, when I was broken from exploring the activities He had forbidden because they were dangerous, when I had grown weary with trying to do what I'd never had the strength or wisdom to do, He came after me and caught me up in His arms. He brought me safely home to His castle and adopted me once again as his daughter.

I am royal again by His compassion.

And now I sit each morning in His Sonlight. We share a bagel and a cup of coffee. He dries my tears or winks at my amazement when I discover even the smallest of His wonders. I chat quietly with my Father, who also happens to be…the King.

NOTES:
[1] Psalm 139:14.

See Questions and Activities, page 228.

Your Turn

*Ask a question, record a thought, sketch a picture, compose a song,
make an argument, draw a cartoon, pen a poem, or write a prayer.*

If nothing comes to mind, just turn the page.

The   Move
Master's

He   across   only   squared

looks   not   eight   squares,

but   cubed   Sitting   yet

infinitely   cubes.   quietly,   perceiving

multi-   ally,   makes   opening

dimension-   He   His   move:

"Knight   C3."   smiles   touches

to   He   but   no pieces.

His   moves   its own   and

knight   under   power   volition.

The   Master   the game,   each

Chess   designs   planning   move:

but He empowers the king
            to move with confidence
and regal wisdom
            in any direction;

He emboldens the queen
    to leap bravely
across the colors

                as far as she wishes;

He equips the knight
    to march down   wisely-plotted,
        strategic paths;

He encourages the rook
    to take far-sighted
  expeditions   to all four points
    of the compass;

He enlightens the bishop,
  sending him
    on unique
      diagonal
        missions;

And He enfolds the humble pawn
  in   loving

    His   embrace

and   by

  trudges his side,

step   slow

  by   step.

Your Turn

Ask a question, record a thought, sketch a picture, compose a song, make an argument, draw a cartoon, pen a poem, or write a prayer.

If nothing comes to mind, read on.

Breathe . . .

I can't keep up with the surprises this week. The schedule was packed to begin with, and then a couple of meetings and a presentation squeezed themselves onto my calendar. It was tight, but doable...until my daughter wound up in the hospital for a couple of days. Now that she is home and the crisis has passed, I am left with the aftermath.

I am trying to pick up the pieces, but nothing wants to be crossed off my list. It seems that even the simple tasks have all become more complicated than they should have been. Traffic is more backed up than usual; none of my passwords work the first time I type them in, so I have to slow down and repeat them one finger at a time; I stop to check the location of a meeting and... "Rats! No cell service!" I've been ten minutes behind on everything today because I just can't find enough minutes to complete one task before I'm already late for the next. My adrenalin is pumping.

As I walk hurriedly across campus, God whispers, "Breathe . . ."

What If...?

A sixteen-year-old dies in her bed when a drunk driver smashes through the wall of her LA home.[1] Successive years of drought spread famine across Yemen, South Sudan, Ethiopia, Kenya, and Somalia.[2] After a brave and painful fight, the mother of six and grandmother of seven succumbs to cancer, leaving her family to wrestle with grief.[3] A spark from a passing trailer ignites the tinder of drought-stressed grass near Redding, California, killing eight and reducing more than a thousand homes to unidentifiable ash.[4] Political antics in Washington shut down the government, leaving hundreds of thousands of unpaid federal workers wondering how to pay their mortgages and buy groceries.[5] A homeless family in Colorado shivers under a tree at the edge of a parking lot, begging for food. A rogue virus sweeps across the globe killing, thousands, and imprisoning billions in their homes.

Bad things happen.

Bad things happen, but we don't expect them.

They make the news. We see them as anomalies, exceptions, interruptions in the normally healthy and peaceful flow of our lives. We expect our days to go along as planned, and most of the time they do. Of course, we experience assorted common annoyances and setbacks, but most of these are not life-shattering events. Even our "bad days" present problems from which we can usually recover and move on. Life goes on pretty routinely, and we see that as normal.

Normal is…paychecks coming regularly so our bills are all paid, maybe even with a little left over for a nice dinner out. It is an unpleasant exception the day a husband comes home early to announce that he has been laid off.

Normal is…rising from a good night's sleep to take a shower, get dressed, and head off to whatever is on my "to do" list for the day. It is an unhealthy exception when I wake with the stomach flu and run toward a toilet to throw up, then stagger back to bed to spend the day moaning with fever.

Normal is…my son going off to school each morning and returning home after classes to complain about his homework. It is an unimagined exception when the phone rings and the voice on the other end reports: "Ma'am, your son has been in an accident."

Normal is…shopping in open and fully-stocked stores, attending social events, family gatherings and church services, and seeing children off to school each morning. It is an unprecedented exception when our economies and our habits are interrupted by the ripple effects of a pandemic, leaving us struggling to find or replace our regular routines.

When really bad things occur, they are invasions. This is not fair! The unexpected attacks our expectations. This is an assault. Tragedy infiltrates the normal and causes unwanted havoc. Why do bad things happen? Where is God?

But what if our whole presumption about how the world works is upside down? What if everything we assume to be normal is, in fact, the exception. What if evil really is in charge?
What if….?

Certainly, we can see evidence to back up this hypothesis. Wars and famines rage; accidents and illnesses take innocent victims; anger and divisions undermine good causes. When we look inside, we watch ourselves succumb to greed, lust, pride, selfishness. Even scientists document our slide toward chaos: the Second Law of Thermodynamics suggests that "The entropy (gradual decline into disorder) of the universe tends to a maximum."[6]

The Bible backs it up too. We are told that when Adam and Eve disobeyed God, all creation fell into bondage to corruption,[7] and the earth began to bring forth thorns and thistles and pain and death.[8] Paul tells us that creation was subjected to futility and that it groans in anticipation of being freed from its bondage.[9]

Can it be that a disgruntled demon really does exist and has masterminded a cosmic rebellion? Can it be that if creation is indeed fallen, it has fallen into the hands of this marauding ex-angel, and he really has become its ruler?
Can it be….?

Truly, God was the Architect who conceived and planned this world. He was the Contractor who gathered all the building materials (*ex nihilo*, or "out of nothing," I might add). He was the Builder who paid careful attention to each detail of the construction. He was the Engineer who made sure that each system worked perfectly. He was the Lighting

Technician who hung the sun and the moon. He was the Decorator who chose the color of each flower and the shape of each tree. He was the Designer who formed each bunny and bat and buffalo.

And then He sculpted His final masterpiece: a family of cognitive creatures who bore His own image, and to whom He gave…the power to choose.

It was rightfully God's world in every way. He created it. He owned it. He cared for it. He delighted in it. But it appears that He made one seemingly fatal error: He let these inexperienced creatures decide whether to live out the plan He had devised, or to go their own way. Can it really be true that on that fateful day when Adam and Eve listened to the serpent and decided that they would rather handle things on their own than to do life God's way, everything did actually change?

Certainly, there was no purchase agreement; *satan did not buy the world from God, and God never signed away the title. Rather evil invaded, enticed the citizens to betrayal, subjugated them, and took over. This diabolical creature is not the rightful owner but rather an arrogant and illegitimate dictator. Nonetheless, if he has taken possession, the world is under his occupying rule.

If that is so, then "normal" is nothing like we imagine it to be.

If the one whose sole purpose is to "steal, kill, and destroy"[10] is also making our laws, then injustice is legal. If we answer to the one called "the father of lies,"[11] dishonesty is desirable. If we are under "the destroyer,"[12] devastation should be expected. If the "tempter"[13] or the "accuser"[14] govern us, we stand condemned. If we follow the lead of the "great dragon,"[15] then we are constantly in grave danger. If the devil is the "god of this age"[16] and "prince of the power of the air,"[17] then we are under the reign of malevolence, and evil is, in fact, normal. Bad things happen because that is what our ruler has decreed, and he revels in them.

So, we must then reverse the question: Why do good things happen?

Good things happen because the Creator and rightful Owner of this world did not just walk away. He has not forgotten, and He did not give up without a fight. In fact, He has no intention of giving up at all.

Every morning that we wake up healthy and feeling good is a penetration of evil by the Great Physician; every day when we have enough to eat is our Provider's[18] airlift of supplies to a besieged people; each time we arrive home from our day safe and sound and in one piece, our Shield[19] has protected us; every week that passes without a natural disaster and every quiet evening we share with family is a conquest by the Prince of Peace.[20]

Suddenly, we must view every good thing that happens, to us not as a normal occurrence to be taken for granted, but as a miracle which we can receive only with awe. In the midst of a world in which the basic presumption is bad, good (and Jesus tells us that there is none good but God)[21] penetrates so often that we fail to notice it; we expect it, and we discount it as routine. We experience daily miracles of biblical proportions and we don't even recognize them.

Some wonder then, why vile and violent things still occur at all. If God is capable of infiltrating the evil and thwarting it, but does not do so, then is He really all that good?

Once upon a long time ago, satan won over the world by convincing God's masterpieces to become traitors. The devil was able to take control because we welcomed him and pledged him our fealty. Perhaps, God, too, waits for our consent. Though God holds the power to overcome the evil one, long ago He vowed He would not force us to love Him. He gave us the right to choose.

Already, God intervenes in our affairs so often that we think His good is normal. We feel entitled to that good and think it "unfair" when bad things happen to us. We fail to notice how often He turns terrible tragedies or injustices into good we could never have imagined or predicted. If He interfered every time satan hatched a diabolical scheme against us, we might never notice Him at all. We would think that we were handling things rather well all by ourselves and live under the illusion that we don't need Him. We would never bother to ask Him into our lives.

And so, He awaits our invitation and our welcome. He longs for us to capsize our misplaced loyalties and return our allegiance to the only One worthy of our trust and devotion. He patiently postpones His recapture of His own crown in this world until we return Him to the throne in our hearts. The almighty and already victorious General holds His fire until the day when we join His insurgency. He waits for us to become saboteurs against the evil one, assisting each new offensive by His invading army with every ounce of our energy, enthusiasm, and ability.

Perhaps then, our prayers mean much more than we thought they did. Maybe each time we pray, we secretly unlock a window that satan had sealed shut and open a way for God and His conquering forces to enter into the world the enemy has taken from Him. How often has satan's plan been foiled, allowing us to come safely to the end of our day because someone somewhere has prayed on our behalf, inviting God's intervention? How many evils have we never known were threatening us because God was welcomed by someone around us? How many times have evil things taken place because we failed to invite God to step in?

Often, I feel that my prayers accomplish little. I pray for healing, but my friend remains sick; I pray for safety and provision for my former students in Haiti, but their city continues to be plagued by poverty and civil unrest. I pray for my friends and neighbors to recognize God's presence around them, but the same few people show up for church each Sunday; I pray for protection and peace for the women of India, but brides are still burned and little girls are turned onto the streets every day.

Could it be that each time I pray, God pushes back the evil just a bit? If I hadn't prayed, might my friend have died? Even if she does, do my prayers invite God—to whom the death of His saints is precious,[22]—to saturate her passing in His comfort and blessing? Is God's protective Hand the only reason my Haitian friends remain alive in the chaos that surrounds them and their families? Are the people around me beginning to sense God in a way I can't yet see? Maybe one woman in India was spared from rape yesterday because of my prayer. In his book, *Miracles,* C.S Lewis suggests,

> "When we are praying about the result, say, of a battle or a medical consultation, the thought will often cross our minds that (if only we knew it) the event is already decided one way or the other. I believe this to be no good

reason for ceasing our prayers. The event certainly has been decided—in a sense it was decided 'before all worlds'. But one of the things taken into account in deciding it, and therefore one of the things that really causes it to happen, may be this very prayer that we are now offering. Thus shocking as it may sound, I conclude that we can at noon become part cause of an event occurring at ten a.m....The imagination will, no doubt, try to play all sorts of tricks on us at this point. It will ask, 'Then if I stop praying can God go back and alter what has already happened?' No. The event has already happened and one of its causes has been the fact that you are asking such questions instead of praying. It will ask, 'Then if I begin to pray can God go back and alter what has already happened?' No. The event has already happened and one of its causes is your present prayer. Thus something does really depend on my choice. My free act contributes to the cosmic shape."[23]

If it is true that evil has usurped the throne of my King; that the King has rallied His forces and mounted a counter-attack; that He waits for me to join Him in the fight; and craziest of all, that I can contribute to the battle by doing nothing more dangerous than sitting down with my cup of coffee to pray, then what am I waiting for?

My Lord, you ask for my allegiance—it is Yours. You await an invitation into my life—please, come. You ask me to stand my ground in prayer—I pledge to faithfully intercede against the evil that surrounds us all, whether I can see Your answers or not. Lord, I am at Your service. Come, Lord Jesus, and retake your place as King of a world ruled by Go(o)d.

NOTES:

[1] "16-year-old girl killed while sleeping in her bed when a 'drunk driver' crashed his SUV into her apartment at 80-miles-per-hour," *DailyMail.com*, April 2014.

[2] Sohngen, Tess, "These African Countries May Fall into Famine by 2018," *Global Citizen*, July 2018.

[3] Holly Friberg, September 15, 1966 to January 12, 2020, Pueblo, Colorado.

[4] Sanchez, Ray, "Northern California's deadly Carr Fire fully contained, state officials say," *CNN*, Aug 31, 2018.

[5] "Hundreds of thousands of federal employees are working without pay," *The Washington Post*, Jan, 2019.

[6] Crawford, Mark, "Rudolf Julius Emanuel Clausius," *The American Society of Mechanical Engineers*, April 2012.

[7] Romans 8:21–22.

[8] Genesis 3:18.

[9] Romans 8:19–20.

[10] John 10:10.

[11] John 8:44.

[12] Revelation 9:11.

[13] Matthew 4:3.

[14] Job 31:35.

[15] Revelation 12:9.

[16] 2 Corinthians 4:4.

[17] Ephesians 2:2.

[18] Genesis 22:13–14 ASV (American Standard Version).

[19] Genesis 15:1 and Psalm 28:7.

[20] Isaiah 9:6.

[21] Mark 10:18.

[22] Psalm 116:15.

[23] Lewis, C.S., *Miracles: A Preliminary Study*. Copyright 1947 C. S. Lewis Pte. Ltd. Copyright renewed © 1947 C. S. Lewis Pte. Ltd. Revised 1960, restored 1996 C. S. Lewis Pte. Ltd. All rights reserved.

*Again, the lack of capitalization here is not a typo. In English, we capitalize names. It is a form of honor given to anyone or anything important enough to be named specifically. God receives special honor in our writing, as His name as well as pronouns and sometimes other nouns that refer directly to Him are capitalized, I offer no such honor to the evil one, thus even his name remains lower case.

Your Turn

Ask a question, record a thought, sketch a picture, compose a song, make an argument, draw a cartoon, pen a poem, or write a prayer.

If nothing comes to mind, just turn the page.

Bored with Miracles

What was once an impossibility
        became a rare and awe-inspiring miracle
                on the day Orville was lifted
                        into the clear North Carolina sky.

But now we have forgotten the wonder.
        Now we wait boredly;
                we board boredly;
                        we stow our bags and sit down—boredly.

We stare straight ahead
        or into our phones,
                not even acknowledging the fact
                        that we are defying gravity.

We are no longer thrilled
        to find ourselves
                lifted from the earth
                        and soaring heavenward.

I fear…
        we may have become bored also
                with the One
                        who lifts our souls to heaven.

See Questions and Activities, page 232.

Your Turn

Ask a question, record a thought, sketch a picture, compose a song, make an argument, draw a cartoon, pen a poem, or write a prayer.

If nothing comes to mind, just turn the page.

Too Many Shades of Blue

I met a woman one night who told me she had been all over the world as a "military brat" and later traveled on pilgrimages with a Hari Krishna monastery. She said that she couldn't get too interested in Christian ideas because she had acquired a "bigger view" of God. She called my faith a little box and said God is much too big to fit into it.

Well, that's a statement I certainly can't argue with. God is, indeed, much bigger than any of the ways I can describe Him, but that doesn't mean He has no parameters, no edges. If we refuse to define God because it would mean putting Him into a box, then we can't accept the biblical definitions of who or what He is, nor conversely, of who or what He is not. We then, by default, leave God defined as All—as everything.

If that is so, then there is nothing that is "Not God." Thus, in theory, He must be good and bad, lazy and enthusiastic, evil, just, unjust, beautiful, horrible, brilliant and stupid.

It is as if I said, "Everything is blue." You could argue with me and point out the many other colors around us, to which I would answer, "No, blue is big. I can't define where it stops, so it must encompass all those other so-called colors as well."

If we look at a bright blue sky turning to dusk, we cannot define exactly where the blue turns to grey, turns to black. The blue doesn't end, so it must all be blue. Even the eventual black of the night sky is really just another shade of blue. We can't tell where the blue of the sky fades into the whispy, white clouds either, so white is also just another shade of blue. Since we can't point out the exact spot where it becomes "not blue" the blue never ends. So, I declare again, "Everything is blue."

"No," you say. And you point out purple and red and yellow and green.

"Just additional shades of blue," I respond. You see for me to define "blue" would be to say exactly where it stops being blue. I can't do that because the totality of blue is beyond my understanding. I couldn't begin to tell you how many shades of blue there are, or how many million things can be described as blue, so everything must somehow be a part of blue.

In defining everything as blue, I make this term, "blue" meaningless because to describe anything as blue would not tell us anything new about it, nor help us differentiate one item from another. They are all different, yet they are all blue, so blue doesn't mean anything. We would simply ignore blue and go on describing everything in our lives by our own judgments of purple and yellow and green (since we all know that blue is too big for us to comprehend anyway).

The same is true of God. If we define Him as everything, then speaking of something as part of God becomes meaningless—it tells us nothing new—so we can go on with our business, tacitly agreeing that He is out there, and that He is too big for us to understand. We can keep making our own individual judgements about the smaller things.

By defining God so broadly, we make Him more manageable—or at least more ignorable. You see, the God who is All can't demand anything specific of me, because whatever I choose to do or to be would be within His scope. The bigger-than-the-box God expects nothing of me. He is easy to get along with.

But what if God is not All?

What if God...Is?
    God is Love.
        God is Justice.
            God is Mercy.
                God is Joy.
                    God is Peace.
That would mean that God isn't;
    isn't hatred.
        isn't capriciousness.
            isn't cruelty.
                isn't hopelessness.
                    isn't discord.

Then He could ask me not to hate or be cruel and capricious. He could call me to love truly, to hope, to care. What if God really is Holy and Perfect? That means He could ask me to strive toward holiness and perfection as well.

All of a sudden, this God isn't manageable anymore. He can't be ignored or defined away. This God is scary.

This God expects something of me.

This God expects everything of me.

As C.S. Lewis notes, this God is "not a tame lion."[1] Does this ferocious beast really love us? And what does such a fierce love look like? Feel like? Lewis writes:

> "If God is Love, He is, by definition, something more than mere kindness. . . . When Christianity says that God loves man, it means that God *loves* man: not that He has some disinterested . . . concern for our welfare, but that, in awful and surprising truth we are the objects of His love. You asked for a loving God: you have one. Not a senile benevolence that drowsily wishes you to be happy in your own way,...but the consuming fire Himself."[2]

This God doesn't wait for us to be beautiful
>>or smart,
>>>or wise,
>>>>or happy,
>>>>>or industrious,
>>>>>>or successful
before He loves us. He loves us now. But because He loves us, He entices us, draws us, demands us to be the best that He knows we can be. He won't stop pushing us
>challenging us,
>>changing us,
>>>teaching us,
>>>>developing us,
>>>>>re-creating us,

until we are beautiful and wise and joyful—until we are, excellent. Until we are, in fact, holy.

That is the God I serve. Not a god who fades into the blue, disappearing into the great amalgamated "All," but the God who truly Is. This God loves me so deeply that He who is without limit was willing to step into my box to become like me, so that He could remake me to be like Him:

HOLY!

NOTES:
[1] Lewis, C. S. 1898-1963 and Pauline Baynes. *The Lion, the Witch, and the Wardrobe*. New York, NY: HarperTrophy. 1994. Originally published in 1950.
[2] Lewis, C S. *The Problem of Pain*. New York: Macmillan, 1962.
Originally published in 1940.

See Questions and Activities, page 233.

Your Turn

Ask a question, record a thought, sketch a picture, compose a song, make an argument, draw a cartoon, pen a poem, or write a prayer.

If nothing comes to mind, just turn the page.

Breathe again . . .

I've been sitting with my notebook in my lap for quite a while, scribbling my thoughts, my questions, and my observations on the page. Then my own messy script catches my eye and I reread what I have written. It is as if God is directing me to go back, saying, "Look at this again."

I realize that I have written something I didn't know before. I stop in the sudden awareness of fresh insight. God has taken over the pen, and I have learned something new in the middle of my own paragraph—or was it my paragraph?

Malchus

*So he asked them again, "Whom do you seek?" And
they said, "Jesus of Nazareth." Jesus answered, "I
told you that I am he. So, if you seek me, let these
men go." This was to fulfill the word that he had
spoken: "Of those whom you gave me I have lost
not one." Then Simon Peter, having a sword, drew
it and struck the high priest's servant and cut off
his right ear. (The servant's name was Malchus.)
So Jesus said to Peter, "Put your sword into its
sheath; shall I not drink the cup that the Father
has given me?"*

John 18:7–11

We sometimes remember Peter as a coward for his
denial, as, I suspect, he did himself until Jesus
forgave and reinstated him on the shore of the Sea of
Galilee. However, it was the same Peter who was afraid to
identify himself with Jesus in the courtyard of the high
priest, who, just a few hours before, had faced an armed
cadre of soldiers in the garden "with lanterns and torches

147

and weapons."[1] In that moment, he was not only willing to claim Jesus but pulled out his one little sword and struck in His Lord's defense. Peter was ready to fight for Jesus in an uneven battle that would likely have ended in his death or arrest. That doesn't seem so cowardly to me. Yet the story of Peter's brave, though somewhat reckless defense also leaves me wondering: What about the man he struck?

The target of Peter's blow was the high priest's servant; some translations call him the high priest's slave. Who was he, and why was he there? Was he ordered to go to bolster the party's numbers even though he would rather have stayed home to get some much-needed sleep?

Or did the servant tag along of his own volition? Life as a servant, even for a high official, probably wasn't all that interesting, and Judas' offer to turn in Jesus no doubt created an unusual level of excitement and intrigue in the high priest's household. Maybe he was just following along for macabre entertainment.

Or did he build his own identity on whom he served and share his master's disdain for this man who thought He could tell the people about God even though He was outside the official religious hierarchy? Maybe the high priest so trusted this servant that he put his underling in charge of the arrest party to make sure that nothing went sideways in his clandestine operation to get rid of this itinerant thorn in his side. After all, the high priest probably had good reason not to trust Judas very far; a traitor who turns once might just as easily turn twice.

And why did Peter strike *him*? Did Peter perceive him as a leader in the group and thus, an obvious first target in a fight? Maybe he just happened to be standing closest to Peter.

More importantly, what happened to the servant after

this eventful night during which he had a front-row seat on the most world-shaking arrest in history? After this crazy weekend was over, and all the buzz about this Jew who was executed (some said as a criminal; others as an innocent; others went so far as to claim they had killed the Messiah) had died down, maybe the high priest's servant just went back to being a high priest's servant. He may have lived out the rest of his days doing whatever high priest's servants were expected to do.

Maybe. But I don't think so.

Luke adds to the story that the man's ear was not only cut off but also healed. Jesus put a quick end to the ensuing fight.[2] Then, in the middle of being arrested and facing all He knew was to come, Jesus paused to touch the man's head and restore his ear—the ear of the man who, for whatever reason, stood among His enemies.

John pauses here in his telling of the story to note that, "The servant's name was Malchus."[3] Why did John care enough to name him? Why should we care what his name was? The story never mentions him again. This was just some inconsequential servant to the evil leader who ordered Jesus' arrest. In modern movie terms, he was an expendable on the wrong side—the side of the "power of darkness"[4] (Jesus' words in Luke's account).

Yet, Malchus is among a handful of the people whom Jesus encountered during His time on Earth whose names we know. We know the disciples, but then, they were major players. We know Mary Magdalene and the other women who went to the tomb on Easter morning. We know Bartimaeus and Zacchaeus and Nicodemus, but we don't know the names of the woman at the well, Jairus' daughter, the rich young man who asked Jesus how to gain eternal life, or the leper who returned to say thank you. Their names are forgotten by history (though not by God). Yet we know the name of this servant, and he has been remembered in many languages for two thousand years each time John's gospel account of Jesus' arrest is read anywhere in the world.

Could it be that for John's contemporary readers, this man was not an incidental aside? Perhaps Malchus was not, as we presume, an expendable who no one remembered or cared about. Maybe, though he stood on the wrong side that night, he was a man about to cross the line.

Did he remain in the garden long after the soldiers had bound Jesus and marched away, and the disciples had fled? Did he look down at the blood drying on his fingers and remember the lightning bolt of pain as the sword slashed by his face? Did he reach up in amazement to touch the ear-made-whole-again? Did he stand in wonder as the recipient of an unprovoked blow followed by an unrequested and completely unimaginable miracle? Could such an experience fail to change a man?

Perhaps he didn't watch the rest of the circus that night. Maybe he slipped home to recount the tale to his wife, who might not have believed him except for the trail of blood that stained his robe from his shoulder to his hem. Did he listen in horror the next day to the scuttlebutt about Jesus' trial and flogging and crucifixion? Was he fascinated and puzzled by the rumors that circulated the following week claiming that this strange Man, whose touch had taken away his pain and left him whole, had healed his own crucifixion wounds and risen from the dead?

Could he, like Nicodemus, have slipped out in the night a few weeks later after the fuss had faded to find one of Jesus' disciples and ask the pointed question, "Who was this Jesus—

really?" Was Malchus standing in the crowd around Peter on the day of Pentecost? Did he hear his long-forgotten childhood language spoken and join the throng of three thousand who found faith that day?[5] Was he, unbeknownst to his high priestly boss, a part of the fellowship of believers in Jerusalem who prayed and broke bread together?[6] Was the healing of his own ear merely the first of many miracles Malchus witnessed as he hung out with the apostles through whom "many wonders and signs were being done."[7]

Did some of those who initially read John's gospel know him well, not as an enemy who stood on the other side and helped to kill their Lord, but as a brother with whom they served that same living Lord side by side? Perhaps Malchus' name is written because he was a slave who became a brother, just as we, who satan attempts to enslave and to slay with his sword of evil, are also brothers and sisters with Malchus and with one another in the blessed fellowship of the One who heals. Will we one day stand next to Malchus before the throne singing, "Holy, holy, holy?"

I look forward to shaking his hand…

. . . and maybe having a look at that ear.

NOTES:
[1] John 18:3.
[2] Luke 22:51.
[3] John 18:10.
[4] Luke 22:53.
[5] Acts 2:4.
[6] Acts 2:42.
[7] Acts 2:43.

See Questions and Activities 234.

Your Turn

Ask a question, record a thought, sketch a picture, compose a song, make an argument, draw a cartoon, pen a poem, or write a prayer.

If nothing comes to mind, read on.

When the Extraordinary Fits

The year after I was born, so was The Doctor. Well, he wasn't born exactly, but rather created as an eccentric time traveler in a weird TV show called *Doctor Who*[1] that has, contrary to any reasonable expectation, continued to be a cultural phenomenon for as long as I have been around (and with much greater fame and popular recognition). Though we have apparently occupied the same space/time continuum, this imaginary individual and I share little else in common—except…the TARDIS.[2]

The TARDIS is The Doctor's space/time-traveling, blue police call box (hmmm…Superman is known for ducking into telephone booths as well—what is it about 3x3 foot structures and fictional heroes with a knack for saving the world?) The TARDIS was named by the creators of the TV show as an acronym: it is a "Time And Relative Dimension In Space" machine.[2] On the outside, the TARDIS looks like an old-fashioned British police call booth. If it weren't for the TV series, its image would have faded into nostalgia with the invasion of the cell phone, and no one in the current generation, particularly on this side of the Atlantic, would even recognize it. However, with The Doctor traipsing around the universe in it, infringing on all those barriers of historical time, the image of the aged, blue police box has become timelessly iconic.

What makes the TARDIS more unusual than any average telephone booth are its dimensions. On the outside, it is no more than a few feet square…ahhh, but on the inside, it is immense, perhaps even infinite. Almost everyone who is invited to join The Doctor in its interior exclaims in amazement that it is "bigger on the inside!"

Though I am slightly less eccentric than The Doctor and claim no aptitude for saving the world from a continuing string of threatening disasters, I, too, have a TARDIS: my faith is also bigger on the inside than it appears from the outside.

The images many people carry of Christians, as well as some of the documents, explanations, and doctrines that we have devised in our attempts to define ourselves, may give the impression that Christianity is only a tiny call box, a futile beacon trying to get the attention of a universe that is not listening. What it embodies, however, is far bigger than its facade. From it, I can reach out to communicate with the Dispatcher of the universe and ask for backup when I find myself in trouble. My SOS brings the vast resources of the Engineer who designed the cosmos and all its moving parts to my rescue.

Come…I'll show you. Step into my TARDIS and look around. I hope you won't limit your view to what you expect to see, but will gaze off into the distances that you might not have anticipated were here.

My faith extends far beyond my physical boundaries; indeed, it has to. As a Christian, I am a human being: small, limited, earthbound, and chained to the hours and days that pass in regular intervals here in the twenty-first century. Yet within this humble (and sometimes blue) exterior, I contain eternity. The God of the universe, who lives beyond the bounds of time and space, chooses to dwell here. If the cosmos cannot contain Him, I certainly can't; and yet He lives within my finite life and reaches out with my tiny fingers. He looks at the world through my eyes but sees beyond my sight. He declares that I display His Image, and He presents Himself to the world through my words and actions, knowing that whatever I portray will be oversimplified to the point of inaccuracy.

God's Presence within me is bigger than I am.

Carrying the Creator of the universe can be a bit unsettling at times. I never quite know what to expect from Him. Sometimes I get frightened or anxious or hopeless, and His Presence becomes a comforting calm within. Other times, I become a bit too comfortable and certain that I can handle the current situation—after all, this is familiar territory; I've done this before. Then, God's Presence becomes a gale, stirring up the winds in my soul and whipping my false surety into white capped waves. He asks me to step out onto uncharted waters where something only He can see looms ahead.

God's plan is bigger than my understanding.

Sometimes we present ourselves to the world saying "Christians believe....Christians do....Christians don't...," implying that our faith is merely a set of rules that dominates both the religion and the people who practice it. The "Thou Shalt Not" language seems to chase us around, along with a reputation for using outdated pronouns (thee, thou, thy). Some of those rules are principles that many of us do try to live up to; others are just rules. And they are all rules we inevitably break. Worse, we use them to judge the faith and behavior of those within or to shake our fingers at those without.

In truth, Christian doctrine is a very human attempt to define our faith and provide an identity for the faithful. It exists in a wide variety of forms, formats, and intensities of dogma, but none of them has succeeded in fully expressing the intricacy of God. To manage our lives within the parameters of our faith, we often reduce it to a set of checkboxes: If we do this…and that….and this, then we are good Christians and good people—but it is never that simple. Those rules cannot make us good nor adequately circumscribe the reality of our faith. God mediates between us and Himself, not by a set of arbitrary rules, but with a perfect balance of justice and grace.

God's good is bigger than my rules.

God loves us, though we often don't do as He asks, and He loves through us, even knowing that our feeble attempts to love often result in damage and hurt instead of the intended ecstasy of involvement with each other. Sometimes we inflict pain, and we don't even care. Although His capacity to love exceeds ours, He continues to plant its seeds in this garden of selfish individuals. Each day He patiently cultivates us, growing us until we bloom with His passion, and the fragrance of His affection infuses the breeze all around us.

God's love is bigger than my capacity to care.

I am not smart enough, nor strong enough, nor fast enough, nor grand enough to contain God's extraordinary Spirit. He is forever spilling out, spilling over, expanding my walls to their breaking points, pressing me to become more than I am. Yet, when I sit down to converse with this all-encompassing Essence who holds tenure in my soul; when I let go of the checkboxes and rules and parameters; when I stop describing His good exclusively by my doctrine and allow myself to recognize His quintessence beyond definition; when I invite His love to infiltrate and inflate my own; I find, amazingly, that He fits.

It seems that I, too, am bigger on the inside than I appear on the outside.

But I am nothing special—just one of billions of people struggling through the daily difficulties of living. Yet, the TARDIS of my faith transports me into the grandeur of the throne room of heaven. It lands me in vast fields of grace through which I am invited to walk. It propels my thoughts into the depths of the stars and transcends my own time, connecting me to brothers and sisters from all of history. It involves me in forever.

Though The Doctor is only a fun fantasy, God is a reality who truly is beyond Time and Relative Dimensions in Space. In communion with Him, I step beyond the temporal and the terrestrial to touch eternity, and I am charged with the task of delivering the potential for that eternity to a world that sometimes can't see beyond the walls of its tiny blue box.

Inside the TARDIS of my FAITH, the extraordinary truly fits—even fits comfortably—inside my ordinary.

NOTES:
  [1] *Doctor Who* is a long running television series owned by BBC Studios; created by Sydney Newman.
  [2] "TARDIS." *Wiktionary, the Free Dictionary*, September 2019.

Your Turn

Ask a question, record a thought, sketch a picture, compose a song, make an argument, draw a cartoon, pen a poem, or write a prayer.

If nothing comes to mind, read on.

Acceleration

Time accelerates:

Minutes become flashes;
    days pass like hours;
        years become brief visits
            into the fleeting present tense.
                Tick........tick....tick...tick..tick-tick-tic-ti-t-t-t.

As I wind down
    like an old grandfather clock,
        time sprints toward my finish line,
            fleeing away into the past and the future,
                threatening to leave me in the dust.

When I was a kid, days dragged on
    especially in the last hour before school let out
        or in the back of the car
            on the way to Aunt Tina's house;
                "Are we there yet?"

Now, no day contains enough minutes.
    My "to do" list spills into the wee hours.
        To accomplish its urgent requirements
            my feeble candle burns at both ends;
                my time grows short.

A Breath of Fresh God

I can no longer control the speed
    or even the direction.
        I am not in charge…
            I discover that I never really was;
                    it's God's road and God's ride.

Can I trust Him at this speed?
    Am I brave enough
        to rev this temporal hot rod
           up to a hundred miles an hour
                  and let go of the wheel?

See Questions and Activities, page 236.

Your Turn

Ask a question, record a thought, sketch a picture, compose a song, make an argument, draw a cartoon, pen a poem, or write a prayer.

If nothing comes to mind, just turn the page.

Breathe deeply . . .

I am catching a quick lunch in the cafeteria, eating hurriedly as I worry about my next class and wonder how I am going to get all my students' essays graded by tomorrow. My mind shifts to regretting a poorly handled conversation when I didn't recognize the person who stepped up to speak to me out of his usual context. Then I recall yesterday's phone call with my son who is struggling in a faraway state where I can do little to help him. I remember an appointment this afternoon and find myself going over my schedule again.

Abruptly, I am dragged out of my spiraling cogitation when my eye catches a young man standing up from a table across the room. His back is to me, and in big block letters across his shoulders, his jacket reads, "BLESSED."

I have no choice but to agree: "Yes, Lord, I am. Thank You." My world is put back into its proper perspective.

A Magnum Opus

A young woman asked me, "What is it like to be married more than thirty years?" How shall I answer her?

I cannot say what it is to others. My answer cannot be an objective analysis—scholarship made relevant by a large sample or a control group. It is an anecdotal study of one case; yet it is a life's work—actually two lives' work—a collaborative magnum opus.

It is to be with someone with whom I share so complete a trust that no thought must be hidden away as unspeakable. It is to disagree and make a case with no concern that dispute might damage the relationship. It is to examine together a controversial issue, looking at it deeply from one angle, then turning it over to delve as deeply into another facet, and another…trying to understand—to truly understand—from all angles, like examining a diamond through a jeweler's glass. It is to speak what is politically incorrect, question the conventional wisdom, and be met only with "Why?" and "What does it mean if you're right?"—even if he doesn't think

163

I am. It is to vote on opposite sides in an election with no condemnation, but rather an understanding of why each of us chose as we did. It is to respect even when we differ.

This marriage will be survived by four very special people, each holding parts of both of us, and yet inaugurating something new and wholly their own. They are offspring of this marriage, the parts of us that proceed into a future we will not know, but they are not this marriage. This is a joining comprehended only by us and by God. It is an integral connection on so many levels that the ties become tapestry, drawing their sources from each of us but weaving themselves into something different than—more than—either.

I am more than myself because I have walked next to him for over thirty years. I can identify traits that are deeply held elements of who I am, but which I learned, adopted, soaked up, and marinated in because they are parts of him. We do not share all the same likes, dislikes, pleasures, fears, desires, hopes, or concerns, but we know each other's likes and dislikes and pleasures and fears and desires and hopes and concerns. With that understanding, we can bring each other the most unique and pleasing gifts and shield each other from the things we fear or which hurt and upset us.

He is not perfect…of course, neither am I. At times I see his flaws and want to correct him. Other times, I am brought up short when he says something that seems beyond any wisdom he could reasonably possess. I am most impressed by his strength when he kneels next to me to pray. He is not God, but he mirrors God for me, reflecting Christ's light into my darkness at times when my own vision has grown dim.

Before the rest of the world, all of us must have a bit of social care, not stepping on other people's toes, being on time, following formal schedules, saying thank you. We must take care what we say, or when not to say. With him I have the freedom to laugh, to cry, to jump up and down on my soap box, to growl in frustration. We can speak or sit together side by side in the car for hours in comfortable silence.

Although we listen to different music, are enthralled by different movies, and are enticed by a variety of different foods and activities, we can step into each other's passions and enjoy them together. We are both richer for the experiences we draw each other into. Without him, I would never have attempted a fourteener climb, and I would certainly not have reached a summit without his patience, planning, and encouragement, and yet I have the memories of seventeen summits. He would not have gone to Ireland if I hadn't wanted to go, so we shared a fabulous, magical trip through the British Isles, delighting together in scenes we never would have imagined on our own.

Compromise brings, not the loss of our own way, but the enrichment of sharing each other's ways. I have let go of things I might have done because they didn't fit into my life with him. He has done the same. Yet, there are so many adventures I would never have recognized as available, possible, or present without being able to look at the world through his eyes. I'd have missed so much laughter, so many surprise kisses, so many silent jokes and quiet understandings shared only between us over the heads of a crowd.

Our society chases the beautiful, the well-built, the sexually accomplished. It touts being "good in bed." I cannot say whether he is nor whether I am, only that we are. Sex between us encompasses not just the physicality of pleasure, but also the intensity of heart and the passion of spirit. It becomes deeper, more passionate, more all-consuming as we grow older. No amount of sexual prowess nor sculpted beauty could compare or substitute for the sweetness of what we share. The young can claim sex all they want—real sex is for the old who have known each other for so many years and shared each others' bodies to such an intense degree that two truly have joined to be one. Sex isn't something we get from each other, but a gift given with complete desire for the other's pleasure and satisfaction—so complete that when we receive that same enjoyment from each other it remains, even after many years, a joyous surprise; a wondrous present simultaneously given and received.

This sensual gift is something that we could not have unwrapped with a succession of partners. He cannot be traded for another man, however young, powerfully built, or sexually expert. Nor can I be exchanged for some perfect-bodied young woman. We are we. We are what and who we are together. To replace either of us would be to take a critical component out of a tried Mercedes engine and trade it for a shiny, state-of-the-art Mustang part—the surrogate may be newer, higher-tech, faster, more powerful, but if it worked at all, it would always be a substitute, a jury rig. It would never purr like the original.

Over thirty years ago we committed to each other and to God. Since then we have shared a grand adventure, made decisions we weren't smart enough to make, walked roads in which we could see only the next step (or the cliff). Through it all we have held on to each other and trusted God to hold on to both of us.

I am his and he is mine and we are His.

See Questions and Activities, page 237.

Your Turn

Ask a question, record a thought, sketch a picture, compose a song, make an argument, draw a cartoon, pen a poem, or write a prayer.

If nothing comes to mind, just turn the page.

Naked
and Unashamed

In my very human
marriage, I can stand
before my husband
naked
and unashamed,
but can I imagine
walking up the aisle
of heaven's Cathedral
wearing nothing but
my faith? I am
afraid it might be
neither complete nor
substantial enough to
provide adequate covering:
just a thin, whispery shroud,
quite easily seen through. I fear
I would be naked and very much
ashamed. I
would tug it
around me,
clutching it
to myself,
but still, it
would not
be enough.
Can I stand
before the
God of all
the universe
wearing
nothing but this?

Dress me, Lord, in a rich and elegant faith,
sewn from the fabric of your grace,
so that I may stand before You no longer naked,
because I am unashamed.

Your Turn

Ask a question, record a thought, sketch a picture, compose a song, make an argument, draw a cartoon, pen a poem, or write a prayer.

If nothing comes to mind, just turn the page.

Forget the Fig Leaves

After Adam and Eve had eaten the fruit of the tree of the Knowledge of Good and Evil in the third chapter of Genesis, God came looking for them, but they hid among the trees. He called for them. Adam finally fessed up and answered, making an excuse, "I heard the sound of you in the garden, and I was afraid, because I was naked, and I hid myself."[1]

"Who told you that you were naked?" God asked.[2]

Adam didn't answer the question. He went on to spill the whole story (blaming Eve, of course), but the issue of his nakedness didn't come up again until the end of the chapter when God made garments of animal skins to clothe them.[3]

That still leaves us with the question: Who *did* tell Adam he was naked? Sort of sounds like a silly question. If I were standing under the trees in the park and my clothes suddenly disappeared, I wouldn't need someone to tell me that I was naked and exposed for the world to see; I would know. And hiding would be high on my priority list.

170

Most interpretations of this story suggest that Adam wasn't suddenly naked. He'd been naked all along, but he hadn't *known* that he was naked until after he ate the fruit. I disagree. I don't think Adam had ever been naked before, and suddenly finding himself so as the result of his disobedience was more than slightly disturbing. Of course, the garments Adam had been wearing before he ate weren't exactly jeans and a t-shirt.

You see, from the moment that God breathed life into Adam, He was concerned with Adam's needs. He planted a garden for him which produced all kinds of delicious things to eat, brought streams of water up to irrigate the garden, and even cared for his aesthetic needs, making sure that the trees were "pleasant to the sight"[4] as well as good for food. He generously gave Adam every seed-bearing plant and all the animals. Then He addressed his need for companionship, forming Eve from one of his ribs so that she would be as much like him as possible, "bone of my bones and flesh of my flesh."[5] God left no stone unturned (or rather, no stone uncreated) in providing for their every need.

I don't think any mention was made of clothing them because Adam and Eve were already dressed. From their very birth (if you can call being formed from the dust being born), "God created mankind in his own image, in the image of God he created him; male and female he created them."[6] They were created to be like the God who had made them and like His Son who, as John 1 makes clear, joined His Father in His creative efforts, for "All things were made through him, and without him was not anything made that was made."[7]

So, if they were created to be so much like the Father and the Son, what were their role models wearing?

God's costume must be pretty spectacular. Psalm 93 tells us that "The Lord reigns, he is robed in majesty,"[8] and Isaiah goes on to describe how "the train of his robe filled the temple" [9] when He sat on His throne. Okay, so the King's robes of majesty might have been a bit ostentatious for the newly-formed man of dust as he worked in the garden.

Maybe Jesus' wardrobe would have been more fitting. After many chapters of scolding about doom and destruction in the book of Isaiah, Jesus shows up to make things right in Isaiah 61. And what is he wearing? "For he has clothed me with garments of salvation; he has covered me with the robe of his righteousness."[10]

So, there we finally have it. Could it be that Adam and Eve were dressed in garments of salvation and covered with robes of righteousness in keeping with the fashion of their Lord?

And yet, we are told throughout the Bible that we, as human beings, have no righteousness of our own. Abraham certainly had none, but thankfully Abraham "believed the Lord, and he counted it to him as righteousness."[11] Paul quotes Ecclesiastes to say that in fact none of us has any righteousness: "As it is written: 'None is righteous, no, not one; no one understands; no one seeks for God.'"[12] He goes on, "For all have sinned and fall short of the glory of God."[13]

Now, I know I'm speculating a bit here, but go with me for a minute.

Perhaps Adam and Eve were not only made in the image of God, but also dressed like Jesus in robes of righteousness, but those robes weren't their own. We humans never had a righteousness of our own because we never needed any. We were designed to share in Jesus' righteousness. The robes Adam and Eve wore belonged to Christ because the righteousness that they had in the beginning was an extension of His, and His robes were designed to fit them perfectly.

Yet, at the moment of their disobedience, Adam and Eve's spirits were diminished; they lost weight. Jesus' robes slipped off because they no longer fit. Adam and Eve found themselves naked, and their children and their children's children, generation after generation, all the way to us, have found ourselves likewise unclothed.

For the rest of human history, we have been searching for some kind of righteousness to cover our spiritual nakedness. We are exposed, shamed, dishonored...and *cold*. We keep trying to cover ourselves up, manufacturing robes out of any scraps we can find, but "We are all like an unclean thing, and all our righteousnesses are like filthy rags; We all fade like a leaf, and our iniquities, like the wind, have taken us away."[14]

And yet, as we stand shivering in the weather, a Tailor beckons. He looks familiar . . . and that robe He is wearing looks very much like the one Adam wore before he fell.

We are told throughout the New Testament that, like Abraham, we can be rescued by faith—that our faith in Christ can be accounted to us as righteousness, and we can be saved from this chilly exposure. "For by grace you have been saved through faith. And this is not your own doing; it is the gift of God."[15] If we embrace Christ, He will clothe us, forgiving all our unrighteousness and dressing us again in His robes, for "There is salvation in no one else, for there is no other name under heaven given among men by which we must be saved."[16]

He promised long ago (maybe on that very day that Adam looked down to find that the robe he had been wearing had evaporated) that "to all who did receive him, who believed in his name, he gave the right to become children of God."[17]

When our faith is counted as righteousness, our own spirits are joined with God's. We become spiritually buff once again, so that Jesus' robes will fit us. In the end, we are dressed as Adam was in the beginning.

You see, in John's vision of the end of the world, he says, "After this I looked, and behold, a great multitude that no one could number, from every nation, from all tribes and peoples and languages, standing before the throne and before the Lamb, clothed in white robes, with palm branches in their hands, and crying out with a loud voice, 'Salvation belongs to our God who sits on the throne, and to the Lamb!'"[18]

Now, that is a fashion trend I can look forward to!

NOTES:

[1] Genesis 3:10.
[2] Genesis 3:11.
[3] Genesis 3:21.
[4] Genesis 2:9.
[5] Genesis 2:23.
[6] Genesis 1:27.
[7] John 1:3.
[8] Psalm 93:1.
[9] Isaiah 6:1.
[10] Isaiah 61:10.
[11] Genesis 15:6.
[12] Romans 3:10–11.
[13] Romans 3:23.
[14] Isaiah 64:6 NKJV.
[15] Ephesians 2:8.
[16] Acts 4:12.
[17] John 1:12.
[18] Revelation 7:9.

Your Turn

Ask a question, record a thought, sketch a picture, compose a song, make an argument, draw a cartoon, pen a poem, or write a prayer.

If nothing comes to mind, just turn the page.

God is near . . .

Quarantined on Easter Sunday, my husband and I "attend" church on both coasts. Using the post-modern phenomenon of live-streaming coupled with the oddity of being in multiple time zones at the same time, we first join our South Carolina congregation from our living room in the mountains of Colorado. Then we drop in on the church where my daughter works in Redding, California. It is kind of fun, but a little disorienting, and still not quite the same as hearing the Easter greeting, "Christ has risen!" and responding "He has risen indeed!" over a hug or handshake.

*And those video Easter lilies?
They have no fragrance at all.*

I tell myself that the beloved scent of Easter lilies perfuming the sanctuary is just another casualty of "social distancing." The following Sunday, however, the pastor of the local Methodist congregation announces "Drive-In Church." We arrive in our car instead of walking (even though the church is only a mile from our house) and back into a parking space just like we used to do at the drive-in movie theater. A makeshift altar occupies the middle of the parking lot, surrounded by enormous Easter lilies.

It is a wonderful service, shared from the safety of my old Buick as we wave at friends and neighbors who are sitting in the comfort of their own vehicles. The pastor speaks into the open air with the assistance of a hand-carried amplifier, and we sing hymns to the accompaniment of piano music wafting out through the open church doors. We even take communion—passed to us through our car window in baggies by purple-gloved hands.

At the end of the service, the pastor announces that these poor orphan Easter lilies are homeless and in need of someone to take them in. I adopt two. They are the tallest lily plants I have ever seen, laden with blooms and covered with buds that promise more blossoms to come. For the next two weeks, those lilies adorn the office from which I teach my college classes over the internet. Again and again, they distract my attention by sending lily-scented breaths of Easter floating across the room, reminding me that God is, indeed, hovering nearby—as close as my next breath.

At 13,000 Feet

I begin my climb, step by steep step, going up and up and further up. I cross and re-cross a stream punctuated by cascading waterfalls. The bright sunlight diminishes as the clouds darken, gradually changing into threatening, swirling shades of grey. The colors of the flowers marking the edges of the trail wash out in the fading light. Then comes the thunder—far away rumbles at first but drawing nearer and getting louder. Suddenly, the rain begins. Will it just sprinkle a little and then clear, or am I going to get really wet? More thunder. This high-altitude hillside is treeless and exposed; it will only become more so as I near the top. Should I go on?

"Lord, should I go on?"

Yes. Go on. I will protect you.

And so, I climb some more. Drops begin to pour down my neck and drip off my nose. The rain turns to tiny hail. Thunder rumbles on. I meet hikers coming off the peak. They are doing what they are supposed to do. Rule number one: when it thunders, get off the mountain. I can see judgement in their faces. They caution me to be careful and continue bailing off the peak.

"Lord should I go on?"

Do you trust Me?

"Am I hearing You? If this is just me doing this, it is foolhardy, but if I am hearing Your voice telling me to continue, then I will go on."

Will you do foolish things if I ask you to? Do you trust Me?

"Yes…I trust You."

And so I keep climbing past more incredulous downhill hikers. More thunder. It is really pouring now. I wipe the water out of my eyes. My shoes are squishy.

"Lord, may I sit under that rock and wait this out?"

Yes.

I leave the trail and brave the muddy slope to a little protected ledge. I sit down, ignoring the puddle of water flowing off the cliff and onto my makeshift seat. I'm soaked enough by now that it hardly matters. I usually hate being wet, but somehow this is okay. I watch the rain and hail pound the rocks as I listen to the crashing thunder.

Finally, the rain begins to subside. The rumbling moves into the distance. A bit of blue appears on the horizon and grows little by little, minute by minute. The rain stops. A marmot waddles out onto a rock below me and looks around. He chirps indignantly when he sees me; I am trespassing on his hillside. For a moment the sun breaks through the clouds and the valley beneath me glows. It is stunning. I take its picture, knowing my camera can't possibly reproduce its glory.

The clouds take over the sun again, but the blue continues to increase. Time to move on. I stand up and bat at my hopelessly dripping hiking skirt. Oh well. I slip and slide my way back to the trail and begin to climb the rock steps again. I cross the creek. More granite stairs. Another switchback, and another. I think of Elijah, who walked forty days for an audience with God. He saw the wind and the fire and the earthquake, and then he heard the voice of God speak in a "low whisper."[1]

Just as I reach the ridge and peek over into the high mountain basin, the sun wins its final battle with the clouds. I gaze into the depths of two emerald and turquoise gems set in the marbled green of the tundra. The wind blowing backward off the retreating storm ripples the water, and it glitters in the newfound sunlight.

I am alone. Everyone else has prudently scurried down the hill in the rain in keeping with due diligence. I sit on a ledge above the lakes as the sun warms the rock around me; my skirt begins to dry. The water trickles. The breeze whispers. A pica squeaks. And I hear in all of it, the still, small voice of God as I sit before the throne. I write a few phrases to describe it, knowing that my word picture can't possibly reproduce its wonder. I give up scribbling and eat a protein bar. Pointy spires across the basin reach toward the few cottony clouds that remain in the sky while the calming lake paints a watery picture of them.

I praise the God who built the mountains, who fills the lakes with rain, and clears the clouds to bring out the sun just for me. I pray that He will help me remember, as I go back home, to keep trusting when I am tempted to turn and run from what He places before me, especially when the threats are less easily identified than lightning. I ask Him to remind me of the thunder and of the sun shining across these glowing, liquid jewels.

My skirt is nearly dry. It's time to head back down the mountain to make dinner on the PocketRocket gas burner back at the tent. I have spent the afternoon in the throne room of my King. His Presence has calmed my heart.

I am content.

NOTES:
[1] 1 Kings 19:12.

See Questions and Activities, page 240.

Your Turn

Ask a question, record a thought, sketch a picture, compose a song, make an argument, draw a cartoon, pen a poem, or write a prayer.

If nothing comes to mind, read on.

Walls Soaked in Prayer

I received an email inviting me to a communion service in a chapel I'd never heard of on the Southern Wesleyan University campus. I had to ask a student where to find it. On reaching it, I realized I had passed by this little church on my way to school every morning, but I'd never noticed it. It was dwarfed by the modern residence hall that sat next to it. The marker called it "Freedom's Hill Church."

My shoes tapped noisily as I climbed the unpainted steps and entered the tiny, wooden-slat building. I slipped into the shadowed interior and took my place on a flat wooden bench that bore the marks of ancient termites. Something about this place felt familiar—maybe its scent? Its essence?

Oddly, I was reminded of my visits to European cathedrals. How could this plain, American antebellum chapel compare with the grandeur of Canterbury or Westminster Abbey? Rather than soaring cathedral towers, its low ceiling hung close above my head. It exhibited no ornate furnishings or streams of stained glass sunlight. Rather than a multitude of candles, two plain oil lamps with dusty glass chimneys burned on either side of the lectern. A rough, wooden cross decorated the front wall. Yet the sense of similarity persisted.

183

I later learned that the little church was originally built in Chatham County, North Carolina. Its abolitionist pastor, Adam Crooks, and his flock suffered great persecution as a result of taking an actively anti-slavery stand in a small North Carolina town a dozen years before the Civil War, but the committed congregation refused to back down. Bullet holes still adorn the church's original door in memory of their devotion to justice and freedom. The building was moved to the Southern Wesleyan campus in 2000 for historical preservation.[1]

Here in this unembellished wooden church, common people who trusted God took their noble stand against the enslavement of fellow human beings. On the bare wooden bench where I sat, they conversed with the same God to whom the cathedral choirs sang. Years of faithful services and sacred Presence had sanctified this space. It needed no pipe organ or famous works of art to mirror the great cathedrals. In this simple place where God has been worshiped by generations, their prayers have soaked into its unadorned walls and polished its hard, wooden pews. Those prayers infused the air around me with the scent and essence of a cathedral.

On that quiet morning, I discovered not so much a breath of fresh God as the lingering scent of the God who has dwelt among those who have gathered in His name for many years, and who still inhabits this peaceful sanctuary. I did indeed discover a sacred place...a cathedral... a place to meet with God.

NOTES:
[1] Southern, Caleb W, "'Silent Witness': Adam Crooks and Christian Holiness Activism," *Southern Wesleyan University*. https://f98a63563fbd4a60c1e3-c47e19be125f47eed9c4ef566904b667.ssl.cf2.rackcdn.com/uploaded/f/0e8842780_1560196637_freedoms-hill-paper.pdf.

Your Turn

Ask a question, record a thought, sketch a picture, compose a song, make an argument, draw a cartoon, pen a poem, or write a prayer.

If nothing comes to mind, just turn the page.

The Chalice

On the night before He died,
Jesus Christ took bread.
He gave it to them,
　　　"Do this in remembrance of me."
Then He took the cup of wine….
"Drink this, all of you."
　　　　　Yes, Lord, in remembrance of You.

Bread is broken; the cup is lifted to heaven,
then passed into my waiting hands.
The King's cup, the Carpenter's cup—the cup of my Lord,
　　　"This is the Blood of Christ; the cup of salvation."
Smooth silver, shimmering gold—heavy in my fingers.
The swirling liquid leaves a thick trace around the bowl:
　　　　　"The Blood of Christ"…*The Blood of Christ.*

Many times, have I drunk from this cup,
His Blood washing over me…through me,
only a tiny sip, yet it drenches like a waterfall,
　　　a cascade of flowing Grace
washing me into the arms
of my God, my Father…
　　　　　Abba.

I have seen my earthly father bleed
as I drove him to the hospital
after the windowpane shattered in his hands.
　　　He warned me he might pass out.
The draining of his blood made him weak;
the flowing of Christ's endows me with strength.
　　　　　This is the Blood of Christ, poured out for me.

Now, I hold His cup in my hand
and gaze into its depths, maroon against gold,
swirling and iridescent in the light.
        "The Blood of Christ,"
His Blood in my hands...
I brush a tear from my cheek.
        The Blood of Christ. The cup of our Salvation.

My brothers and sisters come to the rail.
Having freely received, I now freely give—
the Blood of Christ pouring from my fingertips.
        "This is the Blood of Christ; take it and remember."
I meet their eyes; they touch my heart.
Together, we are engulfed in wonder:
                "The Blood of Christ," *Grace flowing over us.*

The service ends, and I leave the sanctuary.
Stepping through the door into the sunshine,
I no longer hold His cup in my hand,
        but I strive to continue pouring out His Grace
for everyone I meet
because I hold in my heart
                The Blood of Christ...*The cup of my Lord.*

See Questions and Activities p. 242.

Your Turn

Ask a question, record a thought, sketch a picture, compose a song, make an argument, draw a cartoon, pen a poem, or write a prayer.

If nothing comes to mind, read on.

An Invitation to Dine

The invitation surprised me. I had picked up the mail and was casually thumbing through the envelopes: a water bill, an offer for a new credit card, an ad for the local Mexican restaurant, a card with a politician's smiling face asking for my vote, and hmmm…what's this? A creamy envelope edged with gold foil announced "An Invitation to Dine with the King."

It was probably just another restaurant ad, but I was intrigued. I broke the waxed seal and pulled out an elegant, printed card inviting me to "A banquet with the King, 10:00 a.m., Sunday next. No RSVP necessary. Just come as you are."

What could this be? And who schedules a banquet at 10:00 a.m. on a Sunday morning? Curiosity won out. Rather than throwing it into the nearby trash can, I decided to attend.

The day of the feast arrived. I admit I was a bit nervous; I'd never dined with a king before. Who was He anyway?

King of what? I got dressed three times—no, that's too casual; noooo…that one is too flashy—it might draw way too much attention. Finally, I settled on a simple black skirt and a royal blue blouse. I looked in the mirror. Right choice? I guess I'll find out.

Oh, was that a knock at the door?

Oh my! The chauffeur was like no one I'd ever seen before. He looked eight feet tall! His bronze skin gleamed, and his eyes were brilliant like the sun through stained glass. He was dressed in white with a gold belt. He did not speak but bowed politely and motioned toward the…car?

It was shaped like an enclosed horse-drawn carriage, except there were no horses. Its sides showed a lattice work in pale, gold relief decorated with palm trees and pomegranates. The chauffeur opened the back door, and I carefully sat on the carved wooden bench as my attention was drawn to the exquisite stained glass in the car windows. My driver slipped noiselessly behind the wheel.

I'd hardly noticed we had begun to move, when suddenly we were "there." Where, exactly, I wasn't sure, but after coming to a smooth stop, the chauffeur got out and politely opened the door.

I slowly walked up the red carpet—surely this wasn't for me. A doorkeeper, who looked very much like the chauffeur except that she was dressed in deep blue with a similar gold belt, bowed and opened the enormous door. The floor inside looked like cut crystal. Should I walk on it? Could I? Another strikingly tall young man offered me his arm and escorted me inside. I began to wish I'd chosen the fancier dress. We walked down a long hall with walls paneled in cedar, then turned right to encounter another set of beautifully carved doors. They seemed to open by themselves.

I peered inside.

It was nothing like I'd expected. The banquet room held none of the grandeur of the entry way. A long, low table stretched down the middle of the room, surrounded by large brown pillows. It wasn't adorned with carvings. It had no polished veneer. No tablecloth covered its rough wooden surface, and no vases of flowers decorated its length. It looked as if it might have been dragged out of someone's garage or a carpentry shop. Rather than fancy place settings, paper plates and plastic solo cups were scattered across it in no apparent order.

The ambiance also held none of the dignified reserve I'd expected people to adopt for a formal dinner with a king. Rather, it was bright and festive—and a bit loud. The guest were seated on the pillows around the table chattering with their neighbors. They didn't seem to be dignitaries—just a gathering of an unusual assortment of regular people—but each was unique and intriguing. I looked up at my escort. He just smiled and gestured for me to go inside. Still, I hesitated.

Some of the guests were quite old; others were twenty-somethings. A few children played tag in an open area on the far side of the table. Two very pretty blonds with long, straight hair sat together toward the near end of the table. They could have been twins, but were at least sisters. One wore a bright tie-dyed skirt and was figuring with mathematical symbols on a napkin. She seemed to be explaining something to the ponytailed young man next to her. He shook his head insistently and picked up a mechanical pencil and napkin of his own.

The other sister sat sipping her tea, quietly observing

every detail of what went on around her. Though her features bore no hint of anything remotely Asian, she wore a pale pink Indian punjabi. She continued her silent observations until the handsome young man across the table very deliberately gained her attention and began asking her questions.

Not far down the table, a short, squat man in a tattered jacket with stringy grey hair and several missing teeth grinned through his unkempt beard. A multicolored dog of indeterminate ancestry lay contentedly by his feet under the edge of the low table. The bearded guy called out loudly offering everyone who came near a handful of grapes or a drink of his wine. Next to him sat a well-dressed and perfectly groomed executive who carried an air of power and confidence. An iPhone peeked out of his jacket pocket. The two couldn't have been more different, but the suited man leaned his head close to his neighbor and listened until they both chuckled at a shared joke.

A sage with a rounded forehead and a ring of white hair sat near the far end of the group. His face was wizened but animated with interest as he listened intently to the conversation from across the table. Affectionately, he took the hand of the stately woman who sat next to him. She had an expression of permanent amusement on her face. Leaning close, she murmured something in his ear. He let out a deep booming belly laugh that seemed to reverberate off the high ceiling. I wanted to laugh with him.

My tall companion bent over and whispered that I should go on inside. I gingerly tiptoed down the three stairs into the hall, then paused again, still holding the hand railing.

A squarely built gentleman in a skull cap spoke with a distinct Russian accent as he entered into discussion with the fine-featured Middle Eastern man who sat next to him holding the hand of a quiet, dark-eyed girl. The Russian wore a self-assured expression, and their words seemed to grow heated as if an argument was beginning. The girl closed her eyes as her boyfriend grew more adamant.

The debate caught the attention of a tall outdoorsman in black hiking pants and well-worn boots who sat across the table. He gently sipped his wine and listened for a few minutes as their remarks grew louder. A huge, black Newfoundland that had been asleep behind his pillow woke. The dog sat up and pressed his head into the man's free hand, self-petting his own ears until the man gave the dog a final pat and sent him back to lay down. He addressed the men across the table, offering a few quiet words to each. Peace returned, and the girl smiled her thanks across the table.

A sophisticated man with a tight, sharply detailed haircut and a colorful African tunic gestured widely as he described something big to the curly haired young lady blacksmith next to him. Though she wasn't very tall, she was powerfully built and wore a multipouched tool belt around her waist. He accidentally knocked over his plastic cup and, for a moment, looked sheepish. Then they both giggled, and she helped him mop up the mess.

Even as everyone ate and chattered and laughed among themselves, the attention of the guests was often drawn back toward the head of the table. I looked too, and then I noticed…the Host.

He reclined comfortably at the far end of the gathering. He, too, was dressed simply—just a white robe with a rope for a belt—but something about Him was captivating. I could not take my eyes from His face. His skin was the color of sun tea with the light shining through it, similar in tone to the chauffeur and the doorman, but much deeper. His mouth was open in a great smile. His eyes seemed to glow with intensity until He began to laugh—a joyous, infectious laugh. Then His eyes turned to twinkling. He seemed to be enjoying His guests immensely.

I couldn't stand here forever. Trying to be inconspicuous, I inched my way toward an empty pillow at the end of the table nearest the door and began to kneel, but I guess I wasn't discreet enough. The Host, who I later learned was, indeed, the King, caught sight of me.

"Come in! Come in!" He called to me. "No, no. Not down there. Come up here where I can look at you. This is the first time you've joined us for one of our little brouhahas. I'm so glad you have finally come."

Finally come? Was I late? Was I supposed to have come sometime before?

Shyly, I shuffled toward the head of the table. The guests continued to converse; I heard many languages as I walked along the crowd. I could identify Chinese and French and Slovakian, though I couldn't understand what was being said. I caught a few phrases in Spanish and recognized a Russian proverb passing between a thin woman and a boy of about ten.

An empty cushion lay on the floor next to the King. He motioned for me to sit down. I was self-conscious; everyone had seen Him call me forward. What should I do? I had no idea what the etiquette was. I carefully sat down, tucked my feet under my skirt, and smoothed it around me.

Then I looked up cautiously, but no one seemed to expect anything special from me. They continued to chatter together, or with the King. Some drank white wine from their plastic cups and nibbled grapes and cheese from plates that were haphazardly scattered down the center of the table. Others seemed to have glasses of milk and were eating thick slices of brown, grainy bread spread generously with butter and honey. The King smiled at me, but then purposefully turned His attention to someone else, graciously giving me time to gain composure and become more comfortable.

A woman wearing a bright yellow and red shirt and a Green Bay Packer's hat gave me a welcoming finger-wave from down the table. Sitting next to her was a very elderly couple. The old woman, who probably used to be much taller than she now appeared, smiled at me knowingly, not only with her mouth, but also through her faded blue eyes.

I looked around the room. The floor-to-very-tall-ceiling bookshelves that surrounded us stretched into the distance; I couldn't quite tell where they ended. Tightly packed volumes inside all sorts of bindings lined the shelves or lay in jumbled stacks on the floor. Armchairs with lamps were tucked here and there. The room could as easily have been a library as a banquet hall. It seemed as if the sum total of human wisdom was enshrined here. The King caught me looking at the books and smiled faintly. Somehow, I felt sure He'd read them all—or maybe He had written them.

He motioned to the two women across the table from me and introduced us, though I didn't quite catch their names. One was a White woman with an intense gaze but a soft southern accent. The Black woman next to her flipped the fringe from her colorful head scarf over her shoulder and stood up, coming around the table to give me a hug.

"Sister, I'm glad you're here," she said enthusiastically. We exchanged a few friendly words before she went back to sit down.

I looked up and noticed that the ceiling was papered with posters—playbills advertising an array of movies and stage productions in every language imaginable. I recognized

Charlton Heston as Moses and Denzel Washington from "The Book of Eli." I saw an announcement of a British production of "Much Ado About Nothing" and a Chinese play, apparently about a young man and a hawk. It was a colorful myriad of human drama depicting comedy and history and tragedy from all over the world.

The banquet hall was bigger than I had first realized. Were there fifty people around the table? Or a hundred? Or maybe two hundred? More? They seemed strangely uncountable—a multitude that didn't fade into being a crowd, but in which every face retained its distinct personality. The King graciously gave attention to each person, and yet ignored no one else.

A young couple cuddled close together down the table from me. All of their attention was on each other, until the girl teasingly put a grape in the young man's mouth. They both melted into giggles when the King winked at them.

I was not the only latecomer. A tall, thin Black man escorted his wife to a place near the center of the table. He carefully arranged a pillow for her and helped her remove her creamy, wool coat before taking his place by her side. Casually draping his arm across her shoulders, he proudly introduced her as the doctor in the family. She smiled as he quickly got caught up in a discussion with the professor across the table, declaring vigorously that education is impossible without introspection.

Behind them a broad-shouldered young man descended the steps. Leaning on his cane and placing his feet very deliberately, he walked with a pronounced limp. He appeared to be a little unsure, as if he could barely see where he was going. He found his way to the pillow I had tried to sit on at first and sat down awkwardly, picking up his dangling left hand with his right one and carefully laying it in his lap. Once settled, he dived into the conversation, opening with a joke that made everyone around him laugh.

The two young people whose napkins were now fully inundated with mathematical formulas raised their voices. The girl insisted that using multidimensional vectors, she could draw an accurate model of the whole world system. The young man disagreed, arguing that the world couldn't be reduced to numbers. The man whose laughter had shaken the rafters called down the table, adding a new facet to their debate. He told them that, as with musical notes, the real character of the world lay in the space between the numbers. The King interrupted briefly to tell them they were *all* right, and that the numbers and the space between them were, in fact, one and the same.

This fellowship went on for some time, until several new people dressed much like the chauffeur and the door keeper— except their tunics were purple with gold belts—came in carrying a loaf of bread and a bulging leather pouch which, as it turned out, contained a new kind of wine. These were placed before the King who reached out to lay His hand across the top of the bread.

He was joined by two new Persons. Looking at them, I had no doubt that they were family. By Himself, the King had been One to admire—a perfect blending of majesty and familiarity, of the intimate and the extraordinary. Together, these three were completely indescribable, their excellence beyond my words. They stood separately, yet moved in concert. It was as if each knew the thoughts of the others the instant they formed…or perhaps they thought with one Mind.

Gradually, the room grew respectfully silent. The children

returned from their game to sit down with their parents. The King met the eyes of One of the Others and smiled. He picked up the loaf of bread and carefully tore it into small fragments. Lifting the platter of bite-sized pieces high, He said with a great smile: "Take, eat, and be blessed!" A cheer rose from the crowd, and He passed the platter down the table.

The jovial sage continued to smile, but reverently laid his hand on the King's table and closed his eyes before taking a morsel of bread and passing the platter on. Everyone took a piece, joyfully sharing it as they participated in His grand banquet.

The King picked up a silver cup I hadn't noticed before. It was old and somewhat battered—no longer fully round— yet it appeared priceless, reflecting the light that glowed from the faces of the Trio. The King poured wine from the leather flask into the cup. It was a thick, dark burgundy. He lifted the cup toward the ceiling.

"Drink this in grateful remembrance, for you, my children, were dead and now you are alive again; you were lost and now you are found." The cheering was even louder this time. Finally, I understood. This wasn't the King of a country or an empire. He was Sovereign over all that is, not only Master of this table, but of all tables. Yet even more astonishing, this was my King...and my Father.

The King's Son reached out a deeply scarred hand and took the cup from His Father. As I watched, He lovingly started down the opposite side of the table, offering a sip of the rich, red wine to each person He came to. It must have taken a long time for Him to greet everyone on that side of the table and then to come back down my side, but it didn't seem long at all.

With each person, He stopped, looked into their eyes

and smiled as if they were the only one in the room. Some looked self-consciously at their feet, then raised their eyes to meet His with a look of wonder and joy. Others reached out to gently touch His Face. A few threw caution to the wind, wrapping their arms around Him in an elated hug, and He laughed with them.

At last, He came to me. I had been growing more and more excited with anticipation as I watched Him come nearer and nearer down the table, but as He finished with the person before me, I suddenly began to remember…the mess I'd selfishly left for my husband to clean up; my pride in getting my project accepted over my colleague's; the harsh words I'd had for my daughter; the trip to Europe I had been coveting and scheming to finance; the smoldering anger I'd nurtured against my sister. Suddenly, I wasn't so sure I belonged here.

Could I face Him? I looked at the floor.

He waited patiently for a moment. Then He placed a gentle finger under my chin and lifted my face toward His. He looked into my eyes. No, He looked into my soul. Suddenly I knew that He knew all about those things, and they were all forgiven. He smiled. I knelt, looking at Him in awe. He offered me a sip of wine; it was sweet, and I could feel its burn as it flowed over my tongue and down my throat, washing away all that had gone before.

The joy in the room overflowed. People abandoned their places at the table and began stirring around the hall, chatting in excited groups of threes and fives. The King moved easily in and out of these circles adding His comments to one conversation here and another over there. I noticed that some people were sipping from steaming mugs of coffee and wondered aloud where the coffee had come from. The teenager standing next to me pointed out several urns on a serving table across the room.

"I'll get you a cup," she offered. She navigated through the crowd and returned with a steaming mug of the best coffee I'd ever tasted, along with a molasses cookie. Someone pulled out an old fiddle and began to play it. Instantly, a bongo drum and a guitar appeared out of nowhere, and the dancing began. The King looked on in merriment as He watched His guests swing and twirl and waltz and bounce and hip-hop all over the room.

The celebration continued for quite a while longer— I have no idea how long. Then it was time to return home. I was still a bit shy as I stepped up to shake the King's hand and thank Him for inviting me, but He caught me up in a bear hug instead. He insisted that I should come back again very soon.

As I left the noisy banquet hall, I hardly even noticed the crystal floors. The golden chariot no longer impressed me. I'd been inside. I'd been to the banquet.

Arriving home, I found everything as I had left it, yet nothing was the same. The newspaper and yesterday's mail lay on the table; the mess was still in the kitchen (I was glad my husband hadn't cleaned it up); the dresses I'd discarded in my puzzled dressing that morning still lay strewn across the bed. Life would go on, picking up from where I'd left off. Monday morning would come, and I would go back to work as usual. But that was no longer what mattered—I was His.

I am His.

See Questions and Activities, page 244.

Your Turn

Ask a question, record a thought, sketch a picture, compose a song, make an argument, draw a cartoon, pen a poem, or write a prayer.

If nothing comes to mind, just turn the page.

Emmanuel . . .

Often in my private conversations with God, I borrow the words of others, offering psalms, or poems, or prayers they have written, but which express my own joy or sorrow or awe or need. Sometimes I speak aloud; other times in the private silence inside my own thoughts. Over days or years, as I join into these litanies which originated in someone else's soul, but which give expression to my own, their words become personalized and augmented by my circumstances and struggles, my victories and fears—the cries and jubilations of my own heart mingled with those of the original pray-er.

One Easter, I heard a pastor pray the following prayer (or at least, part of it), which he attributed to St. Augustine of Hippo. I went looking for the text, found it online, and began including it in my own daily prayers. Later, in trying to identify where among Augustine's works it was written, A friend, who is also an expert on Augustine, discovered that no one seems to be entirely sure that it is Augustine's at all.

No matter who penned it, these words beautifully express my own quest to remain constantly aware of God's continual Presence with me.

As I prayed it over time, my heartfelt repetitions gradually augmented the original words with my own petitions, bubbling up in times of elation, of exhaustion, of grief, of frustration, and of wonder at the many ways God has appeared when I had forgotten to expect Him.

In this adaptation, the words of Augustine (or his unknown understudy) are written in regular type, *while my additions are added in italics.*

Prayer to Seek God Continually

O Lord my God, I believe in you, Father, Son and Holy Spirit. Insofar as I can, insofar as You have given me the power, I have sought You. *But* I became weary, and I labored. *I am so easily distracted and overwhelmed.* O Lord my God, my sole hope, help me to believe and never to cease seeking You. Grant that I may always and ardently seek out Your countenance—*Your face, present with me wherever I am.* Give me the strength to seek You, for You help me to find You, and more and more You give me the hope of finding You, *and You come looking for me when I can't find You.*

Here I am before You with my firmness and my infirmity. Preserve the first and heal the second. Here I am before You with my strength and my ignorance. Where You have opened the door to me, welcome me at the entrance *and draw me in to set me on the path You have chosen for me.* Where You have closed the door to me, open to my cry *or lead me past the barred way to the door You have opened instead. Either way, let it be Your path I walk.*

Enable me to remember You*; to see You and recognize You;* to *hear You and* understand*; to follow You,* and to love You *with all my soul.*

Father, I am Yours; hold me. Jesus, I am Yours; send me. Holy Spirit, I am Yours; inspire me.

Amen.[1]

—(Possibly) St. Augustine of Hippo
Italicized portions by Charissa

NOTES:

[1]"Prayers of St. Augustine," Villanova University Mission & Ministry. https://www1.villanova.edu/villanova/mission/campusministry/RegularSpiritualPractices/resources/spirituality/restlesshearts/prayers.html.

Your Turn

Ask a question, record a thought, sketch a picture, compose a song, make an argument, draw a cartoon, pen a poem, or write a prayer.

If nothing comes to mind, just turn the page.

Reader Response

If you have enjoyed reading *A Breath of Fresh God,* please share it with friends either in conversation or on your favorite social media platform.

Please consider posting a review on:
Amazon
GoodReads
or on Charissa's author website at:

charissafryberger.com

Charissa is available to speak to community groups, church groups, book clubs, or other gatherings. She can be reached at:

charissa.e.fryberger@gmail.com

Questions and Activities

Abba

Because you are sons,
God has sent the Spirit of his Son
into our hearts, crying,
"Abba! Father!"

—Galatians 4:6

1) Is it easier to think of God as the Celestial King on the throne or as the Delighted Father who holds you close? Which characterization do you prefer? Why?

2) How have you experienced God's delight in you as His beloved child? What symbol or phrase can you give yourself to help you remember that sense of delight in times of distress or depression?

3) What do you think God's laughter sounds like?

Activity: Imagine sitting in God's lap. Close your eyes and think about how that would feel. What would you say to Him?

Go ahead and tell Him.

The Augustinian Ant

Where shall I go from your Spirit
Or where shall I flee from your presence?
If I ascend to heaven, you are there!
If I make my bed in Sheol, you are there!
If I take the wings of the morning
and dwell in the uttermost parts of the sea,
even there your hand shall lead me,
and your right hand shall hold me.
—Psalm 139:7–10

1) Can you remember a time when you became aware that you had "underlooked" God? What triggered your re-awareness of His Presence? Did the realization make you feel guilty for missing Him or elated to have found Him again?

2) Have you tried to prove God to someone? What approach did you take? How did the other person respond?

3) How can you "add your voice" to the chorus of Christians who have tried to describe their encounters with God?

Activity 1: Find a trail of ants following each other back and forth to their nest. Interrupt their path by placing something in their way. Watch how they behave. Can you imagine God stepping into our path and interrupting our orderly march to get our attention?

Activity 2: Read *The Practice of the Presence of God[1]* by Brother Lawrence or *A Testament of Devotion[2]* by Thomas Kelly. These short reads describe the experience of learning to notice God even in the mundane moments of life. They invite and guide us toward an unbroken awareness of

Him even as we live out all the busyness of our lives. They also counsel us in how to return to such an awareness of the Divine Presence when we discover that we have slipped away and "underlooked" God. Try applying their methods in your own life.

NOTES:

[1] Brother Lawrence, *The Practice of the Presence of God.* Whitaker House, USA, 1982. Original publication date: sometime soon after 1691.

[2] Kelly, Thomas, *A Testament of Devotion.* HarperCollins Publishers. Original copyright, 1941.

Distracted

When Moses came down from Mount Sinai,
with the two tablets of the testimony in his hand
as he came down from the mountain,
Moses did not know that the skin of his face shone
because he had been talking with God.
—Exodus 34:29

1) Do you find it difficult to find God's Presence in the busyness around you? What cue or reminder jogs your memory and reassures you that God is still paying attention to you?

2) Does it comfort you to know that God's Presence and care in your life is not dependent upon your spiritual attention span, but rather on His—that even when you are distracted

from God, He is not distracted from you? How do you recognize and experience His faithful affection and support?

3) Have you ever become aware of God's Shekinah—the glow of His Presence—shining on you? Have you noticed someone else who seems radiant with it? How can you recognize it?

Activity: We usually mark engagements on our calendars or log them into our phones in advance, but Divine appointments have a tendency to happen when we are not expecting them. To log them in our memories, we have to mark them after they have taken place. Open your appointment calendar (paper or electronic) for the past week or two. Look at the events that you had planned in advance. As you think through what actually happened each day, try to remember and identify conversations, incidents, meetings, and surprises that you hadn't planned. Log those Divine appointments on your calendar.

Before the King

Blessed are the poor in spirit, for theirs
is the kingdom of heaven.
—Matthew 5:3

1) What does it mean to be "poor in spirit?" How do you handle that poverty? How does it lead you nearer to God?

2) Can you imagine God in the splendor of majesty? If so, where do you see yourself in that vision of Him?

3) Try picturing yourself as a child resting in God's lap or as a student sitting at His feet soaking in all He has to teach you. Does this change the way you see yourself in relation to Him? How?

Activity 1: Read Psalm 51 aloud. Imagine God cleansing you with hyssop and washing away all your failings. If you are in a group, find a small branch from a bush or tree. Dip it in water and use it to shake droplets over the group in a symbolic cleansing.

Activity 2: Go into a church sanctuary when no one else is there. Walk slowly toward the front and sit down. Imagine God sitting on His throne at the altar with Jesus standing nearby. What would you say to them? What do you think they might say to you?

Start a conversation.

Rivers of Living Water

On the last day of the feast, the great day,
Jesus stood up and cried out,
"If anyone thirsts, let him come to me and drink.
Whoever believes in me, as the Scripture has said,
'Out of his heart will flow rivers of living water.'"
—John 7:37–38

1) What does Living Water look and feel like to you? Does

it ebb and flow around you? Does it rush like a fierce flood, or impeceptibly rise around your toes and up to your knees? Does it feel cold as it reaches your belly?

2) We often describe our encounters with God through the lens of tangible experiences. Which image most closely pictures the Divine Touch as you have felt it: the glow of God's Shekinah light shining around us, the intensity of His Fire burning within us, or the deluge of Living Water flowing through us, over us, out of us? Or can you best describe your experience of Him with a different image?

3) How can you shake God's love all over the people around you like an over-exuberant puppy?

Activity: Get a bottle of cool, fresh water and a clear drinking glass. Look at the water in the bottle for a minute or two. Watch the light shine through it. Look beyond it to see how it reflects and changes the view of things on the other side of the bottle. Imagine its touch and its refreshing taste. Be aware of this life-giving water as God's gift to you.

Now, remove the lid and pour the water slowly into the glass, watching it tumble out and swirl around the edges. Listen to the babble of the water as it flows. Finally, lift the glass and take a long deep drink. Imagine all these sensations being intensified when you drink God's Living Water, infused with His life and power and His deep refreshing love for you.

The Gallery

When I look at your heavens, the work of your fingers,
the moon and the stars, which you have set in place,
what is man that you are mindful of him,
and the son of man that you care for him?
Yet you have made him a little lower than the heavenly beings
and crowned him with glory and honor.

—Psalm 8:3–5

1) Have you ever thought of God as a painter, a jeweler, a weaver, or a sculptor? How does it change the way you view plants, animals, or natural scenes to recognize them as His artwork?

2) Sometimes it is easy to get caught up in the functionality of the world and the demands of the missions God has placed before each of us. A look at the wonder, beauty, and intricacy of what He has created around us, however, quickly proves that He is interested not only in the necessary, but also in the beautiful. How often do you take time not only to stop and smell the flowers, but also to thank the One who designed them?

3) What does it mean to be "curators of His Great Global Gallery?" How can we better serve in this role?

Activity: Go somewhere with a natural view—a park, a beach, a lake, a mountain, a forest trail—or watch from a parking lot as the sunset lights up the clouds. Imagine God actively painting the scene before you. Stand for a while and watch Him work. Notice what colors are in His pallet and whether He is painting with a broad brush and bold strokes or in minute and exquisite detail. You can take a picture of the scene, knowing, of course, that the reproduction won't have the same intensity and power as the original.

Imagine God signing, "I Am" in the corner of the picture. As you turn to go home, recognize that you have witnessed the creation of a masterpiece.

Maybe God will let you choose a title for it.

Eight Billion Pixels

So God created man in his own image,
in the image of God he created
him; male and female he created them.
—Genesis 1:27

1) What do you think of the idea that our image-bearing is a collective act? Does it change the way you see yourself?

2) Do you imagine God through the lens of who you are, or do you see yourself through the lens of who He is? How do these different lenses affect your view of God? Of yourself?

3) Which characteristic(s) of God do you think you are designed to mirror to the world? How can you best communicate these pixels of who God is to the people around you?

Activity: Rather than trying to show the world a complete

image of God through your life (a task at which we must all inevitably fail), choose a trait or characteristic of His which you feel most qualified to exemplify. Write that attribute on a card or sticky note. Keep the note with you through the next week or post it somewhere you will see it, maybe on the bathroom mirror or the dashboard of your car.

As you go through the week, focus on demonstrating that particular part of God's character to the people around you, whether they are strangers, friends, or family members. Look for specific ways to make your life and behavior illustrate your pixel in the vast image of God.

Letters from Abroad

I have looked upon you in the sanctuary,
beholding your power and glory.
Because your steadfast love is better than life,
my lips will praise you.
So I will bless you as long as I live;
in your name I will lift up my hands.
—*Psalm 63: 1–4*

1) Is it difficult for you to turn your experiences of God into words so that you can describe them to other people? How else can you show others what you have discovered about Him?

2) What does it mean to remember those who have gone ahead of us, even if history has forgotten them? Are we impacted by their legacies? What impact might our own legacies have?

3) What do you think God's language sounds like? How can you learn to speak it more fluently?

4) What special graces—miracles—has God provided when you have been traveling? What miracles have you seen Him do when you were safe in your own hometown? In which place is it easier to recognize God's activity around you? Why?

Activity: Think of a place you have always wanted to go. Draw yourself a boarding pass for a flight bound for that location (or make a train ticket, if you prefer not to fly). Hand your boarding pass to a friend, sit down, fasten your seatbelt, and think of what miracles you might hope to see God do on your imaginary journey. In what ways will you need to depend on Him to step in and handle what you can't manage on your own?

Write a letter home.

Ты or Вы?

For you did not receive the spirit of slavery
to fall back into fear,
but you have received the Spirit of adoption as sons,
by whom we cry, "Abba! Father!"
—*Romans 8:15*

1) When you first address God in prayer ("Our Father," "Dear Jesus," "Father God," "Dear Lord," "Papa"), do you

experience God first as Вы or Ты? Do you begin by worshiping in amazement of the One whom Rich Mullins calls our "awesome God"?[1] Or do you start as if you were sitting down to a chat with a friend? Does your initial approach remain the same throughout your prayer, or does your awareness of Him vary as you speak with Him?

2) Eighteenth century philosopher, Blaise Pascal wrote, "What sort of freak then is man! How novel, how monstrous, how chaotic, how paradoxical, how prodigious! Judge of all things, feeble earthworm, repository of truth, sink of doubt and error, glory and refuse of the universe."[2]
Which part of Pascal's description of the nature of human beings do you most often think identifies you? Which do you think most closely describes how God sees you? Why?

Activity: A friend of mine who has walked with God for over eighty years no longer uses common forms of address when she prays. Instead she has adopted the practice of simply calling God "Papa." For a couple of days, try addressing God as "Papa" or "Daddy" when you pray. How does this change the way you talk to Him?

NOTES:
[1] Mullins, Rich, "Awesome God," *Winds of Heaven, Stuff of Earth,* 1988.
[2] Pascal, Blaise. *Pensees.* The Penguin Group, London UK 1966. Original publication date: 1670.

Trip Report: Pikes Peak

Then as he lay and slept under a broom tree,
suddenly an angel touched him, and said to him,
"Arise and eat."
Then he looked, and there by his head
was a cake baked on coals, and a jar of water.
So he ate and drank, and lay down again.
And the angel of the LORD came back the
second time, and touched him, and said,
"Arise and eat, because the journey is too great for you.
"So he arose, and ate and drank;
and he went in the strength of that food
forty days and forty nights
as far as Horeb, the mountain of God.
—1 Kings 19:5–8 NKJV

1) Have you ever climbed a mountain, literally or figuratively? How did the climb change your perspective? Is it an experience you wish to try again, or was one summit enough?

2) From the outset of any mountain trail, the summit appears dauntingly distant and difficult. It is hard to imagine ever standing on the top. When have you plodded toward a goal that seemed impossible at the outset, but proved finally achievable?

3) One complication in climbing a mountain is that when we reach the summit, we are only halfway through the hike; we still have to come back down. In what experiences have you found the aftermath of achieving the goal to be just as difficult as the climb to get there?

Activity: Climb a mountain. If you live in a mountainous

area and you are reasonably fit, go for a hike. If you don't live near any rocks or hills, or your health doesn't permit hiking, find a more symbolic mountain: perhaps a bridge over a nearby river, a grassy hill in a local park, or even a flight of stairs.

Before you begin, look about and become familiar with the scenery around your starting place. Climb slowly. Be attentive to the effort that each step requires. Ask God to make you more aware of His Presence with you as you ascend. When you reach the top, stop and look around. Notice how different your perspective is from where you began.

What tasks or goals in your life are like a mountain climb? Ask God to make you aware of Him walking next to you as you hike up those figurative mountains as well.

Raw Deal

But he said to me, "My grace is sufficient for you,
for my power is made perfect in weakness."
—2 Corinthians 12:9a

1) It would be nice to believe that as we attempt to serve and honor God, He will provide ideal circumstances for us to work in, but this often isn't the case. In Genesis 3:18, God tells Adam that because of his disobedience, the ground will bring forth thorns and thistles to impede his efforts to grow food.[1] Paul later writes to the Corinthians that to prevent him from becoming conceited, God had given him a

thorn in his flesh which God refused to remove despite Paul's pleading.[2] What "thorns" has God put in your way?

2) God tells Paul, "My grace is sufficient for you, for my power is made perfect in weakness."[3] Is it difficult for you to look beyond your difficulties—your thorns—and recognize the sufficiency of God's grace? How can you find ways to trust His power in your weaknesses?

3) For a moment, imagine your life as a poker game. What hand are you holding? Do you doubt that God will make it good enough to win the pot? Do you tend to be surprised when you are dealt a winning hand or disappointed when you lose?

Activity: If you are in a group, cut a sheet of paper into squares and write one physical or circumstantial "thorn" on each square (include such impediments as a broken leg, losing your job, an elderly parent falling ill, a diabetes diagnosis, a house fire, a job transfer to another city, the totaling of your car in an accident, a heart attack, etc.).

Shuffle the papers, then deal them face down: one to each member of the group. Ask each person to take a few minutes to think about how they would continue the life-missions God has given them in light of their assigned "thorn."

Ask group members to share their thoughts.

NOTES:
[1] Genesis 3:18
[2] 2 Corinthians 12:7–9
[3] 2 Corinthians 12:9

Cancer, Comfort, and Calling

"You have heard that it was said,
'You shall love your neighbor and hate your enemy.'
But I say to you, love your enemies and
pray for those who persecute you,
so that you may be sons of your Father who is in heaven.
For he makes his sun rise on the evil and on the good,
and sends rain on the just and on the unjust."
—Matthew 5:43–45

1) Do you find it difficult to balance the need to sit with God praying or reading His Word against the need to reach out to a hurting world with His compassion and care? How can you find a happy balance between the two?

2) In the swirl of disparate views that surround all of us in modern life, how easy is it to love those with whom you disagree? How can you honor them as people whom God loves even if you oppose their opinions?

3) Do you think it is okay to be frustrated or mad at God? How can you reconcile your own desires with circumstances God allows to come into your life that are not what you wanted them to be?

Activity: Think about a circumstance God allowed in your life that was not as you wished it to be. What were the results of that circumstance? List as many good things as you can that came out of what seemed to be a bad situation. It is okay to admit to God if you still wish you hadn't had to go through the trial. If you are in a group, share your stories and their resulting blessings.

To Be or Not To Be the Blind Man

Therefore I will boast
all the more gladly of my weaknesses,
so that the power of Christ may rest upon me.
—2 Corinthians 12:9b

1) Do you ever react to Bible stories with a "Hey, wait a minute!" moment, or does it seem disrespectful to question God's motives? Do you think He minds if we question Him?

2) Does it seem unfair that sometimes we are subject to the consequences of other people's poor choices, bad behavior, or sins? How can you reconcile this unfairness in the world with what you know of God's goodness and justice?

3) Read Romans 8:28. Have you witnessed God bringing blessing out of suffering? When have you seen something unexpectedly good grow out of what seemed at first to be terrible circumstances?

Activity: Next time you sit around the dinner table with friends or members of your family, ask them to share stories of when they have seen God bring something amazing and wonderful out of uncomfortable, unfortunate, or even tragic circumstances.Take notes. Later, summarize the stories into a page or two that you can keep and/or share with others as encouragement when circumstances in life seem to be going sideways.

The Author

Let us run with endurance the race that is set before us,
looking unto Jesus, the author and finisher of our faith,
who for the joy that was set before Him
endured the cross, despising the shame,
and has sat down at the right hand of the throne of God.
—Hebrews 12: 1b–2 NKJV

1) Many fiction writers say their characters argue with them as they write. Do you ever argue with God as He lays out your plot? How do you express your arguments? How does He respond?

2) How would you categorize the book God is writing you into? Is it a mystery, an epic, a fantasy, a romance, a comedy, a drama, a horror story? Might you describe it as a factual documentary? Perhaps it is an action-adventure or a thriller or a fairy tale? Could you be playing the starring role in a work of science fiction? Do you think it will be legendary?

Activity: Most books are divided into chapters. The plot develops throughout those chapters, but each is unique. Some set the stage; others bring in strange, new characters or provide clues to the next twist of the plot. If God is the Author and your life is His story, can you identify the events and stages that make up the different chapters?

Write the Table of Contents for the book that God is writing about you. Title the story and give God the byline. List the chapters that you have already read and give them interesting or descriptive chapter titles. If you can, anticipate any upcoming chapters or end your Table of Contents with an expectant "To be continued…."

The Song of a Lonely King

He brought me to the banqueting house,
And his banner over me was love.
—Song of Solomon 2:4

1) Can you imagine Solomon as a lonely man, despite being surrounded by servants, officials, wives, children and everyone else in the court? Have you ever felt lonely even among people you knew cared about you? How can you overcome that kind of loneliness?

2) How have you viewed Song of Songs when you have read it in the past. Have you enjoyed its poetry and passion, or have you been uncomfortable with its intimacy? Can you identify what feelings it touches?

3) We often think of God's love in the child's understanding that "Jesus loves me, this I know"[1] or in the theoretical conception that "God is love."[2] Does it change your response to Him when you view God's affection for you in terms of romantic love? How is it different to accept God's love if it is intense and personal rather than abstract?

Activity: Go to "Song of Songs NKJV Audio Bible" on Youtube at: https://www.youtube.com/watch?v=2AP3S6oAas8. Close your eyes and listen to this dramatic reading of Song of Songs. Say a prayer to the God who loves you that intensely.

NOTES:
[1] Warner, Anna Bartlett, "Jesus Loves Me," *Hymnary.org*. Original publication 1859.

[2] 1 John 4:8

In the Playroom

Jesus called them to him, saying,
"Let the children come to me,
and do not hinder them,
for to such belongs the kingdom of God.
Truly, I say to you,
whoever does not receive the kingdom of God
like a child
shall not enter it."
—Luke 18:16–17

1) Do you find it easy or difficult to see yourself as a beloved daughter or son of the King? What interferes with your ability to identify yourself with His royalty?

2) How well do you take care of the many gifts God has placed in your life? Do you need to be a better steward of them? How can you do this?

3) In what ways do you co-create with God? This may be as big as building a house, as artistic as painting a landscape, or as immediate as making tonight's dinner.

Activity: Gather a box of crayons and a piece of colored paper. Sit at a table or, if possible, on the floor (crisscross applesauce) and imagine one of God's sunsets. Try to recreate it on the paper. When you've finished drawing, close your eyes and ask God to help you with your real-world projects, the creative tasks in your own life. Finish by writing a short psalm about a project on which you plan to collaborate with Him.

The Strong Nuclear Force

He is the image of the invisible God,
the firstborn of all creation
For by him all things were created,
in heaven and on earth, visible and invisible,
whether thrones or dominions or rulers or authorities—
all things were created through him and for him.
And he is before all things,
and in him all things hold together.
—Colossians 1:15–17

1) We sometimes imagine God holding the big things in our world together but forget that He keeps all the little things intact as well. When you think of God holding the atoms together, what does that look like to you?

2) If God is holding the little parts of our physical world together, how might this apply to the routine matters in your daily life? What would it look like to let Him manage your daily tasks, arrange the appointments on your calendar, or keep your problems under control?

Activity: Draw a diagram of an atom with the same number of protons in the nucleus as there are members in your family. Label the protons with the names of your family members. Label the negatively charged electrons that circle outside of the nucleus with the things that cause disagreement or anger among you. Pray for your family, acknowledging the repelling forces that threaten or weaken your relationships. Invite God to draw you together and sustain your family with His Strong Force.

An Audience with the King

Therefore take up the whole armor of God,
that you may be able to withstand in the evil day,
and having done all, to stand firm.
Stand therefore, having fastened on the belt of truth,
and having put on the breastplate of righteousness
and, as shoes for your feet, having put on
the readiness given by the gospel of peace.
In all circumstances take up the shield of faith,
with which you can extinguish
all the flaming darts of the evil one;
and take the helmet of salvation,
and the sword of the Spirit,
which is the word of God.
—Ephesians 6:14–17

1) Does the image of God as our King resonate with you? Can you relate to Him on the throne in great majesty, or does such a metaphor make Him too distant, unapproachable, archaic, or undemocratic?

2) What do you think of the medieval practice of praying before the altar in a prostrate position? What modern position or practice might help you recognize or experience the power and eminence of God?

3) Are you comfortable with seeing yourself in the role of the knight going out to fight for your King? What other role might better describe your relationship with God?

Activity 1: Close your eyes and pray. Imagine God on the throne and recognize Him as your King. Pledge your loyalty to Him. Promise Him, in grateful response to His mercy, that

227

all of the life He's given back to you, all of the abilities He has bestowed on you, all of your possessions, hopes, and dreams are at His disposal. Thank Him, not only for the majesty He displays as your King, but also for the love He shows as your Father.

Activity 2: Read Ephesians 6:14-17 (previous page). Draw a picture of yourself wearing the armor of God, but modernize it so that each piece looks more like something you might actually put on rather than something you might find in a medieval museum. For example, rather than a metal helmet, what might you wear that could symbolize God's protection of your mind and thoughts? What sort of shoes or belt might you choose? Instead of a sword, what might be your weapon of choice to represent Gods Spirit?

Breakfast

This is the day that the LORD has made;
let us rejoice and be glad in it.
—Psalm 118:24

1) What does it mean to "sit in adoration of this great Creator King?" What comes to mind when you adore God?

2) What can you identify in your own history that was a rejection of your position as prince or princess? Have you apologized to God for this treason? If not, take time to tell Him you are sorry. Recognize that He accepts your apology.

Activity: Set a nice breakfast table with two plates and two mugs. Depending on your tastes and habits, place a pitcher of cream, a sugar bowl, some cream cheese, a dish of butter, or whatever other condiments you like in the center of the table. Arrange some flowers in a vase for decoration— they might be cut flowers from a florist or grocery store, blooms from your garden, or even dandelion blossoms you've gathered from your lawn. Cut a bagel or pastry in two, laying half on each plate. Pour both mugs full of coffee or tea or whatever beverage you prefer.

Open your Bible and read Psalm 118:19–29 aloud. Then enjoy breakfast with your Father, the King.

The Master's Move

Many are the plans in the mind of a man,
but it is the purpose of the LORD that will stand.
—Proverbs 19:21

1) The format of this poem makes it difficult to read until we figure out its shape and get the hang of reading outside our habitual line-by-line pattern. We must decipher it before we can begin to find its meaning. Sometimes our Bible passages must also be deciphered before we can begin to understand their meaning. How do you approach this biblical decoding exercise?

2) As pieces on God's chessboard, we live in a fragile balance between moving "under our own power and of our own volition," and trusting the Chess Master to design the game and plan the next move...and the next. Do you ever find yourself

arguing with God over what the next move should be? What leads to such arguments? How do you resolve them?

3) Would you like to play chess with God—with Him, that is, not against Him?

Activity 1: If you know how to play chess, find a partner and play a game. Pay attention to what it takes to see beyond the next move and plan a strategy that builds on past moves and even on past mistakes. Thank God for His foresight and farsight in laying out our paths before us.

Activity 2: If you don't know how to play, find a YouTube video of someone playing chess. Watch the intensity of the players' concentration. Thank God for His unwavering attention and concern for everything that happens in your life.

What If...?

Be still before the LORD and wait patiently for him,
fret not yourself over the one who prospers in his way,
over the man who carries out evil devices!
Refrain from anger, and forsake wrath!
Fret not yourself; it tends only to evil.
For the evildoers shall be cut off,
but those who wait for the LORD shall inherit the land.
—Psalm 37:7–9

1) Do you see good things as "normal?" When bad things happen in your life, do you tend to see them as unfair? What do you think of the idea that our understanding of "normal" is upside down?

2) How does our inability to know the impact of our prayers affect the way you pray? Does it discourage you from praying? Or does the thought that your prayers may have influence far beyond what you can see energize your prayer life?

3) Do you believe that our prayers are effective, even when we pray for big things that affect whole cities or countries? In what ways have you seen God answer big prayers?

4) Do you agree with C.S. Lewis when he suggests that our prayers, even if offered after the fact of an incident, can contribute to the "cosmic shape?"

Activity: Make a list of all the good things that have happened in your life this week. This could be as simple as, "I had a great breakfast this morning." Choose one of those good things and think through all that must have happened to bring about that event. Consider the people who contributed to it, the resources that went into making it happen, and the timing that was necessary to bring all those people and resources together.

For example, my wonderful breakfast required the eggs and the chickens that laid them, the farmer who grew the wheat for my toast, the trucker who brought food to the grocery store, the clerk who sold them to me, my husband who washed the frying pan last night, the electric cable that provided power for my stove to cook the eggs, as well as the people who put up those electric lines.

Thank God for coordinating so much good into your life.

Bored with Miracles

By the word of the LORD *the heavens were made,*
And all the host of them by the breath of His mouth.
He gathers the waters of the sea together as a heap;
He lays up the deep in storehouses.
Let all the earth fear the LORD;
Let all the inhabitants of the world stand in awe of Him.
For He spoke, and it was done;
He commanded, and it stood fast.
*   —Psalm 33:6–9 NKJV*

1) What does it feel like to be bored? Do you wish time would pass faster so you can move on to the next not-so-boring item on your schedule? Would you really want God to shorten the allotment of time He has ordained for you?

2) How can you replace boredom with fascination? Can you become truly aware of the honor God has shown us in allowing us to live each moment?

3) What inspires you to wonder?

Activity 1: Next time you fly, leave your phone off as you wait, as you board, as you take off. Think about what is happening as your plane becomes airborne. Let yourself be awed that mere air can hold a plane aloft. Be amazed that in a few hours you will exit this metal tube to find yourself in a different city, perhaps a different time zone. Thank God for the privilege of flying.

Activity 2: If you don't have an opportunity to fly, choose any situation in which you need to wait in line. Resist the urge to check your phone. Notice the people around you. What are you all waiting for? What gift will it have for you or what problem will it solve? Try to be excited instead of humdrum.

Too Many Shades of Blue

Finally, brothers, whatever is true, whatever is honorable,
whatever is just, whatever is pure,
whatever is lovely, whatever is commendable,
if there is any excellence,
if there is anything worthy of praise,
think about these things.
—Philippians 4:8

1) Does God have edges? Do you tend to think of God as All, or do you notice things that are not God?

2) Do you find your relationship with God comfortable and safe, or does He surprise you? Is He ever scary and unpredictable like Lewis' untamed lion?[1]

3) How does God challenge you, change you, teach you, develop you, re-create you, to be beautiful and wise and joyful—to be excellent? To be holy?

Activity: Get copies of C.S. Lewis' famous books from the Chronicles of Narnia: *The Magician's Nephew* and *The Lion, the Witch, and the Wardrobe*. First read chapters 8, 9, and 10 in *The Magician's Nephew*; then read chapters 7 and 8 in *The Lion the Witch and the Wardrobe*. Read aloud (with someone else if possible) and listen to Lewis' portrayal of Aslan, the character who represents Christ in the stories. What do you think of the way Lewis pictures him? Do you think Jesus is safe, or is He, as the beaver says, "Not a tame lion?"[1]

NOTES:
[1] Lewis, C.S., *The Lion the Witch and the Wardrobe*, 1950

Malchus

Therefore, if anyone is in Christ, he is a new creation.
The old has passed away; behold, the new has come.
All this is from God, who through Christ
reconciled us to himself
and gave us the ministry of reconciliation;
that is, in Christ God was reconciling
the world to himself,
not counting their trespasses against them,
and entrusting to us the message of reconciliation.
—2 Corinthians 5:17–19

1) Why do you think John pauses to name Malchus?

2) Do you ever see yourself as an extra or an expendable in the epic story God is writing? What might help you remember that He knows your name?

3) We don't only step across the line once when we commit to following Christ. God asks us to do it over and over each time He calls us farther out of our comfort zones in His service. What surprises or miracles have caused you to step over one of those lines?

Activity: Think about the next thing that God is calling you to do for Him? It could be as immediate as taking dinner to someone who is hurting or as big as stepping into a whole new mission field. When you have made a choice to do what He is leading you toward, place a line of tape on the floor. Stand on one side of the tape and pray; tell God what you hear Him asking you do to. Commit yourself to the task.

Then step across the line.

When the Extraordinary Fits

For by grace you have been saved through faith.
And this is not your own doing; it is the gift of God,
not a result of works, so that no one may boast.
For we are his workmanship,
created in Christ Jesus for good works,
which God prepared beforehand,
that we should walk in them.
—Ephesians 2:8–10

1) We sometimes say that contemplating the vastness of God makes us feel small; yet the idea that God lives in us implies that we are immense—indeed, bigger on the inside than on the outside. Which do you feel most often, small or immense? What thoughts lead you to this feeling?

2) How can you step outside the constraints of rules and checkboxes to let your faith expand into its full dimensions?

3) Do you find the idea that God lives within you to be comforting, or a bit unnerving? Does He sometimes do things from within that you don't expect? That you don't like? Is it sometimes difficult to let Him be God from within?

Activity: Stand in front of a mirror. Look at your own dimensions. See yourself as a telephone booth: small, simple, self-contained, ordinary. Then close your eyes or turn your back to the mirror and ask God to show you your soul with its vast spiritual potential, its complicated and interwoven relationship with God, and its unique and extraordinary design. Try to appreciate who God has made you to be and who He is continuing to fashion you into, despite your apparent limited dimensions.

Acceleration

And those who know Your name
put their trust in You;
For You, O LORD, have not forsaken those who seek You.
—Psalm 9:10

1) Time is an inescapable dimension of our human environment. Do you experience time as a comfortable constant which governs the regular routines of life? Or as a variable that seems to get faster or slower depending on the urgency of the task at hand? Or as a competitor in a race which always seems to be one step ahead of you? Or in some other way?

2) How is God's view of the world from outside time different from our own temporal view? How do you think our perceptions will change when we step out of time to join God?

3) How can you practice trusting God so that you can learn to let go of the wheel?

Activity: Choose a morning or an evening or a couple of hours when you don't have any time-centered obligations to anyone else. If you can, take down the clocks where you are or turn them toward the wall. Set aside your phone and computer or put a sticky note over the place on their screens where they show the time. Try to go about your business without knowing what time it is or how much time has passed. Focus on the tasks you are doing, what is going on around you, or what is happening within you instead of on how long it is taking or what needs to be addressed next. How does ignoring time for a little while change your activity, your sensation, or how you approach what you are doing?

A Magnum Opus

You shall no longer be termed Forsaken,
Nor shall your land any more be termed Desolate;
But you shall be called Hephzibah, and your land Beulah;
For the LORD delights in you, And your land shall be married.
—*Isaiah 62:4 NKJV*

1) Does thirty years sound like a long time to be with one person? Do you think you might become bored with him or her? Why? What might prevent that boredom? If you have been married a long time, what keeps your relationship fresh and real?

2) If you are married, how has your marriage changed you?

3) Having someone we trust completely is important, whether we are married or unmarried. If you are single, do you have a friend or family member with whom you have the freedom to laugh, to cry, to jump up and down on your soap box, to growl in frustration, or to sit in comfortable silence? Who is that special person? If you don't have a friend like that, how could you develop such a trusting relationship?

Activity: Find a couple who has been married for a long time. This may be an older couple in your family, your church, or even a local assisted living center. Ask them if they would tell you about their marriage. Ask questions to get them started: What first attracted you to each other? What do you remember most from your first year of marriage? How are your relationship and your feelings for each other different now than they were then? How has God participated in your marriage? What is the best thing about being married for so many years?

Naked and Unashamed

I will greatly rejoice in the LORD;
my soul shall exult in my God,
for he has clothed me with the garments of salvation;
he has covered me with the robe of righteousness,
as a bridegroom decks himself like a priest
with a beautiful headdress,
and as a bride adorns herself with her jewels.

—Isaiah 61:10

1) Have you ever felt naked before God? What caused the feeling? What relieved it?

2) Does the picture of your faith as a garment resonate with you? If not, what other symbol for faith seems more illustrative? Why?

Activity: Look at yourself in the mirror. First, see yourself as you do every day when you get ready to leave your house. Primp a little: fix your hair; touch-up your makeup; straighten your shirt. Gradually try to stop noticing your flaws. Intentionally turn your attention away from the blemish on your cheekbone, the extra pounds you are carrying, the eyes you've always thought were too close together, the grey in your hair. Try to see yourself as God sees you. Look for His designs in your appearance and in your personality.

Thank Him for who He made you to be.

Forget the Fig Leaves

After this I looked, and behold,
a great multitude that no one could number,
from every nation,
from all tribes and peoples and languages,
standing before the throne
and before the Lamb,
clothed in white robes,
with palm branches in their hands,
and crying out with a loud voice,
"Salvation belongs to our God
who sits on the throne, and to the Lamb!"
—Revelation 7:9–10

1) Why do you think Adam was embarrassed and hid when he discovered himself naked; after all, no one was around to see him but God and Eve? (Incidentally, take the word "embarrassed" apart by syllables to get a stronger sense of the meaning of the term).

2) What are you spiritually wearing today? How might looking forward to the "fashion trend" described in Revelations change your figurative fashion choices now?

3) What would a "robe of righteousness" look like? Would you think of it as formal or casual wear? What might you choose as accessories to wear with it?

Activity: Draw a design for your robe of righteousness. Decorate it to suit who you are. It is Jesus' robe, loaned to you, but He appreciates your individuality. What symbols might you trim it with to express who you are in Christ and/or who you want to be in relation to Him.

At 13,000 Feet

Then He said, "Go out, and stand
on the mountain before the LORD."
And behold, the LORD passed by,
and a great and strong wind tore into the mountains
and broke the rocks in pieces before the LORD,
but the LORD was not in the wind;
and after the wind an earthquake,
but the LORD was not in the earthquake;
and after the earthquake a fire,
but the LORD was not in the fire;
and after the fire a still small voice.
—*I Kings 19:11–12 NKJV*

1) Has God ever led you to do something that seemed foolish by the standards of reason? Were you afraid? How did it turn out in the end?

2) Have you altered the usual routines of life to do something special for someone you love? Can you imagine God changing the normal patterns of the world or rearranging circumstances just for you? How would that make you feel?

3) We often think of miracles only as startling events or answers to big problems such as making a blind man see or feeding five thousand people or maybe healing someone of cancer. Do you think something as simple as the sun coming out from behind a cloud at just the right moment can be called a miracle too? What little daily miracles have you experienced?

Activity: Sit somewhere alone, out of doors if possible. Don't do anything; just sit. Let yourself be aware of your surroundings. What do you hear? Try to separate and name each sound. Describe to yourself the colors of the things you can see around you—not just blue and green and yellow, but what shade and intensity of blue or green or yellow. Feel the air on your face and on the exposed parts of your body. Is it still, or can you detect a breeze? Does it feel cool, or a little too warm? What scents is it carrying to you? Imagine that everything around you furnishes and decorates God's throne room.

Sit quietly with Him for a while. What do you think God may be whispering to you in the view? In the wind? In the sound of the bird singing above your head? In the quiet of your own heart? Write down what you think He is saying.

Walls Soaked in Prayer

Therefore, since we are surrounded by
so great a cloud of witnesses,
let us also lay aside every weight,
and sin which clings so closely,
and let us run with endurance the race that is set before us,
looking to Jesus, the founder and perfecter of our faith,
who for the joy that was set before him
endured the cross, despising the shame,
and is seated at the right hand of the throne of God.
—Hebrews 12:1–2

1) Have you ever experienced the essence of one place in another? How was God a part of the essence you sensed?

2) Do you think your prayers can soak into the walls and inhabit a place, or do they evaporate after you have spoken them, to be remembered only in the mind of God?

Activity: Sit silently in a church sanctuary. Look at the walls, the décor, the symbols, the chairs. Think of the people who have sat there before you. What might they have prayed about? Did they shout and praise in grateful joy over all God had done for them? Were they ill and praying for healing? Were they celebrating a birth or mourning the death of a loved one? Did they ask God to provide because they were unemployed and didn't know how their needs would be met? Did they sit in quiet contemplation or sob as tears flowed unchecked down their cheeks? Embrace their prayers as they soak into your own and sanctify your time here. Let your prayers mingle with all the prayers that have been lifted there before.

The Chalice

For I received from the Lord what I also delivered to you, that the Lord Jesus on the night when he was betrayed took bread, and when he had given thanks, he broke it, and said, "This is my body, which is for you. Do this in remembrance of me." In the same way also he took the cup, after supper, saying, "This cup is the new covenant in my blood. Do this, as often as you drink it, in remembrance of me."
—1 Corinthians 11:23–25

1) The communion service we share evokes the images of Jesus' violent death. Viewed objectively, it is, at best, a little weird; at worst it is rather ghastly. It has horrified observers since it was practiced by the early church, yet it carries for us intense meaning and illuminates the central event or our faith. How do you personally experience this sacrament? What meaning does it hold for you?

2) Do you ever find that church rituals such as communion become routine? Sometimes we go through the motions merely because we have gone through them before. How can we make them fresh and find new awareness of their depth and meaning?

3) What does it mean to hold the cup of our Lord in our hearts? How can we demonstrate this to those around us?

Activity: Next time you receive communion, pause before you drink from the cup. Look deeply into the wine or juice it holds. Note its color. If you can, swirl it around and notice how it moves in the cup. Thank God for what Christ's blood bought for you and for the privilege of sharing in His communion.

An Invitation to Dine

They devoted themselves to the apostles'
teaching and the fellowship,
to the breaking of bread and the prayers.
And awe came upon every soul,
and many wonders and signs were being done
through the apostles . . .
And day by day, attending the temple together
and breaking bread in their homes,
they received their food with glad and generous hearts,
praising God and having favor with all the people.
And the Lord added to their number day by day
those who were being saved.
—Acts 2:42–43; 46–47

1) Do you imagine a banquet with God as a perfectly decorated formal dinner where the table is set with beautiful china and each delicious dish is presented as a work of culinary art, or more like a garage get-together with Solo cups and fingerfood where the wine might get spilled on the floor and mopped up with napkins? Which type of party can you imagine God throwing? Which would you be more comfortable attending?

2) With which character around the table do you most identify? Why?

3) Most of us have taken communion many times. Does the thought of receiving it directly from Jesus' hand seem exciting or intimidating? Or maybe it brings up a different emotion?

4) Does the image of God as the fun-loving Host who laughs and dances with His guests seem natural to you, or maybe a bit irreverent? Why?

Activity: Share an "Agape Feast" with a group of friends. Sometimes translated as "charity," *agape* is the most broadly defined of the Greek words for love. It is often used to express God's love for us, as well as the unconditional, selfless, all-encompassing love we hope to share with each other. Christians have used the term "Agape Feast" to describe a simple meal shared among believing friends who come together for fellowship and prayer. Often it consists of fingerfoods like fruit, cheese, crackers, and sweet breads. Abandoning electric lighting in favor of abundant candles adds an intimate, festive sense to the Agape Feast.

Recommended Readings

Inspirational and Devotional Reading

The Practice of the Presence of God by Brother Lawrence
A Testament of Devotion by Thomas Kelly
A Year with C.S. Lewis by C.S. Lewis, edited by Patricia Klein
Christmas Stories and the Christmas Story by James Campbell
The Well by Mark Hall
The Very Next Thing by Mark Hall
Epic: The Story God is Telling by John Eldredge
Even the Sparrow by Jill Weber
*Devotional Classics: Selected Readings for Individuals and
    Groups* edited by Richard Foster, and James Bryan Smith
The Confessions of Augustine by St. Augustine

Stories

The Great Divorce by C.S. Lewis
The Screwtape Letters by C.S. Lewis
The Magician's Nephew by C.S. Lewis
The Weeping Chamber by Sigmund Brouwer
The Holy War by John Bunyan
The Presence by T. Davis Bunn
The Book of Hours by T. Davis Bunn
The Shack by William Paul Young
The Robe by Lloyd C. Douglas
The Curate's Awakening by George MacDonald,
    edited by Michael R. Phillip
Paradise Lost by John Milton

Thank you!

Any act of creativity is a collaborative effort, both because we create in concert with God, and because other people share in bringing our ideas to realization. Many people have participated in making a *A Breath of Fresh God* happen. I am grateful to each for their contributions and encouragements.

My most important human creative partner is also my partner in life. My husband, David, lets me bounce ideas off of him, reads and edits drafts, draws me back if I get a little too far out, and listens as I struggle. He also steps in to reconcile us when I get into fights with my computer. Although nothing I have written here could have been possible without his faith, support, and years of inspiration, "Magnum Opus" is a special tribute to the blessing he is in my life.

Our four children, Miriam, Alyssa, Aspen, and Emory also provide both inspiration and the questions that make me step back, take a breath, and reconsider my experiences from new angles. Each of their unique perspectives adds facets to my own thinking and sharpens my view of God and the world.

The idea that eventually became *A Breath of Fresh God* grew out of reading *Christmas Stories and the Christmas Story* and *The Holiness of Water* by my friend and mentor, James A. Campbell. His willingness to spend many hours in honest, no-idea-off-limits discussions with me has contributed not only to my writing, but also to my thinking and to my awareness of God. Jim often reminds me that God laughs with me, and that He is not only the Creator, but also the Appreciator of beauty. My favorite piece in the book, "An Invitation to Dine," was inspired by Jim and written for him.

Although the idea for this book began long beforehand, writing a portion of it as the creative thesis for my master's degree at Clemson University turned it from a dreamed-of idea into a real and doable project. Dr. Andrew Lemons, my thesis advisor and chair of my graduate committee, was willing to step with me out of academic convention. He encouraged me to explore thoughts and experiment with literary forms that do not usually appear in a thesis. Andy is a man of letters, both in the traditional sense of the phrase and in his literal love for writing long missives. The inclusion of "Letters from Abroad" and "The Augustinian Ant" were both due to his encouragement.

Martha Brown has been my second in dozens of projects; in other endeavors, I have been her second. She is truly a friend with a deep heart and a sincere faith. She has listened over coffee in her kitchen as I have struggled through the stages of writing and has offered her comments and per-spective on various drafts and versions. "An Audience with the King," which was first written as a speech that I delivered for a coaches' event during our Prairie Frog Challenge speech and debate tournament and later used as part of a Chautauqua performance by our beloved F.R.O.G.s, is dedicated to her.

My book editors, Lisa Stilwell and Paul Schleifer, did a fantastic job of helping me clean up the book manuscript and clear it of awkward spots that failed to communicate what I meant to say. Lisa's expertise and encouragement, as well as her willingness to coach me through some of the publishing conundrums that were outside my experience, went above and beyond the job of an editor. Paul's choice to test out my discussion questions and activities by answering them all gave me much needed insight into how someone outside my own head might understand the questions.

Jenna Yeager offered her artistic talents and technical skills to fill in the visual and graphic holes in my giftings. She designed the book cover and masterminded my website (and probably prevented me from outright murdering my computer). I am also grateful to my sister, Annette Meserve Lucero, who is an outstanding artist and designed the wind graphic used on my "breath" pages.

None of us who write or speak can know if the message we intend to send is the same as the message that is received in the mind or heart of those who read or hear it. The gift of perspective was provided by my many colleagues and friends who read my work at various stages, offering their comments and suggestions. Thank you to Josiah Dasher, Quin Friberg, Laura Yeates, Carole Poysti, Chelsey Friberg, Brenda Zane, Pricilla Hill, Robert Underwood, Scott Bailey, Martha Brown, Paula Pruden-Macha, Barb Musso, Emilie Sons, Michelle Tennant, Kathy Hall, Ikenna Ezealah, Rev. Justin Hare, Jane Wilson, Betsy Thraves, Fr. Bob Menard,

Cheryl Watson, Dr. Ronald Anderson, and Sarah Watkins. My sister, Maureen Meserve, was also always ready with a word of encouragment.

At times, I have needed to get away to sacred places where I can separate from the distractions of life to pray, find inspiration, and collaborate with God. Many of the pieces in this book were written or refined at *The Potter's Place*, in Central, South Carolina or *The Easy Yoke Ranch* in Beulah, Colorado. Thank you to Don and Shannon Schaupp and to Ron and Sandy Anderson for their dedication to making such sacred spaces available, both to me and to the many others who have found God's peace in these very special retreat centers. "Walls Soaked in Prayer" is dedicated to them and to their missions.

Finally, I want to thank my parents, Clyde and Jan Meserve. Their influence in my life extends far beyond this book. They encouraged my writing from childhood and taught me not to discount dreams and ideas, but to jump in and try whatever I feel led to do.

Patron's Page

Special thanks to those who contributed the funding that was required to bring *A Breath of Fresh God* to print. Their confidence, encouragement, and support have been gifts to me and have served critical roles in making this book a reality. Many thanks to:

Martha and Paul Brown

Clyde and Jan Meserve

Dr. Aaron and Terren Wilson

Brenda and Stewart Zane

Veronica and Mark McKay

Sue and Ron Martin

Karen Pickering

Neil and Cheryl Watson

Don and Satia Schwarz

Dr. Ron and Sandy Anderson

Barbara and Donald Musso

Scott and Michelle Tennant

Jackie and Russell Figgins

Dr. Randolph and Leah Johnson

Carole and Charlie Poysti

Heather and Byron Ward

Jim and Maggie Campbell

Harvey and Katie Fryberger

Carol and Rich Myers

Joy Dasher

Paula Pruden-Macha

Scott and Alicia Bailey

Grace Prevenient

Kimbra Birchler

Coreen Kelley

Kathi and Jerry Seay

Kay and Joe Corbo

David Fryberger

Rachel Deibler

Laura and Jeff Yeates

Scott Williams

Ann Harris

Nathan Anderson

Maureen Meserve

Dr. Jonathan Sircy

John and Kathy Hall

THANK YOU ALL!

About the Author

Charissa Fryberger and her husband, David, live in wonder at the plot twists and surprises God weaves into the story of their lives. Whether they are climbing the mountains near their home in southern Colorado, exploring the forests of South Carolina, dropping in on any of their four adult children, or adventuring in some out-of-the-way corner of the world, they often catch a breath of fresh God in some unexpected place.

Charissa wrote her first "book" in a blue-lined school notebook when she was in the fourth grade. She published her first poem in the seventh grade and by age sixteen was working as a stringer for the local daily newspaper. She published articles, poetry, and essays throughout her college years. After they were married, David offered her a tremendous gift: the opportunity to write full-time while he provided the family income. For the next two years, she freelanced for magazines and literary journals.

With the birth of their first daughter, followed in rapid succession by three more babies, writing took a twenty-five-year pause while Charissa and David raised, educated, and loved four dynamic young characters through the opening chapters of their own stories. After working herself out of a job as a homeschool mom, Charissa decided to go back to school herself, earning a master's degree in English at Clemson University. She went on to teach English and public speaking as an assistant professor at Southern Wesleyan University in South Carolina.

Their adventure in following Christ continues as Charissa and her husband explore far and near from "basecamp" at their family home in Beulah, Colorado. Everywhere they go, Charissa finds new chapters to write about the transcendent, yet intimate God in whose footsteps they follow.

Charissa is available to speak to community groups, church groups, book clubs, other gatherings.

She can be reached by email at:

charissa.e.fryberger@gmail.com

See Charissa's website at:

charissafryberger.com

TIMELINE OF WRITINGS

1985	Charissa and David meet at the University of Wyoming.
1987	After much struggle, Charissa chooses to follow Christ.
	Charissa and David are married.

"The Gallery"

1988	They move to Ponca City, OK; Charissa writes full-time.
1990	They move to Houston TX; Miriam is born.
1991	Alyssa is born.
1993	Homeschooling begins.
1994	Aspen is born.
1996	The family moves to Beulah CO; Emory is born.
1997-2000	During three temporary job assignments, they explore California, Washington, and Oregon.

"The Chalice"

2004-2015	Charissa coaches the FROGs (the Front Range Oratory Group speech and debate team) and teaches homeschool history and literature classes.

"An Audience with the King"
"Forget the Fig Leaves"
"Before the King"
"Too Many Shades of Blue"

2012	The family spends a sabbatical semester in Philadelphia PA.

"The Strong Nuclear Force"
"What If...?"

2015	With Emory's graduation, the Fryberger homeschool is closed.
	Charissa teaches briefly at an orphanage in Haiti.

"An Invitation to Dine"
"A Stirring"

2016	David, Charissa and Miriam hike into Chicago Basin CO.

"At 13,000 Feet"

David and Charissa travel the British Isles; Charissa continues on to Czechia, Slovakia, and Kazakhstan.

Beulah survives two forest fires.

"Letters from Abroad"

2017	Charissa and David move to Clemson University, SC.

She receives a cancer diagnosis a month into grad school.
>"*Trip Report: Pikes Peak*"
>"*Raw Deal*"
>"*Cancer, Comfort, and Calling*"
>"*The Augustinian Ant*"

2018   Charissa spends five weeks in Prague for TEFL training.
>"*Abba*"
>"*Bored with Miracles*"
>"*Distracted*"
>"*Magnum Opus*"

She returns to Kazakhstan to teach a second time.
>"*Ты or Вы*"

2019   Charissa graduates with a master's in English.
>"*The Author*"
>"*The Song of a Lonely King*"
>"*In the Playroom*"
>"*Naked and Unashamed*"
>"*Acceleration*"
>"*The Master's Move*"
>"*To Be or Not to Be the Blind Man*"
>"*When the Extraordinary Fits*"

She begins teaching at Southern Wesleyan University.
>"*Walls Soaked in Prayer*"
>"*A Fragrance*"
>"*Rivers of Living Water*"
>"*Breathe Deeply*"
>"*Eight Billion Pixels*"
>"*Breakfast*"

2020   Charissa and David weather covid quarantine in Colorado.
She returns to South Carolina when Southern Wesleyan resumes face-to-face teaching.
>"God is Near"
>"*Malchus*"
>"Emmanuel"

2021   Charissa and David move back to Beulah, Colorado.
A Breath of Fresh God is published.

For additional copies of
A Breath of Fresh God,
please contact Charissa at:

charissa.e.fryberger@gmail.com